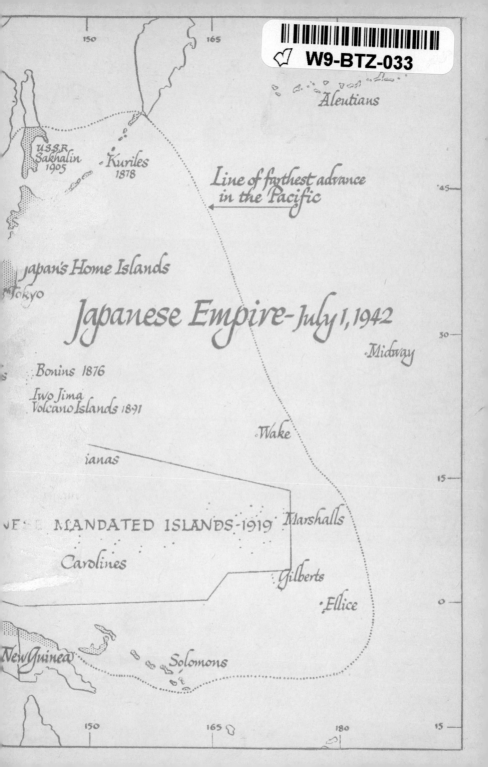

150　　165

Aleutians

USSR
Sakhalin
1905　　*Kuriles*
1878

Line of farthest advance
in the Pacific

Japan's Home Islands

Tokyo

Japanese Empire—July 1, 1942

Midway

Bonins 1876

Iwo Jima
Volcano Islands 1891

Wake

...ianas

...E.. MANDATED ISLANDS—1919　*Marshalls*

Carolines

Gilberts

Ellice

New Guinea　*Solomons*

150　　165　　180

THE FUTURE OF JAPAN

ISSUED UNDER THE AUSPICES OF THE
AMERICAN COUNCIL,
INSTITUTE OF PACIFIC RELATIONS

The Future of Japan

Japan

WILLIAM C. JOHNSTONE

OXFORD UNIVERSITY PRESS
LONDON   NEW YORK   TORONTO
1945

A WARTIME BOOK

TO
ANNE
AND
BOB
AND
BRACE

Preface

To attempt to plot the future of Japan, to evaluate proposals for dealing with this defeated nation before it has suffered defeat, may seem an act of prophetic presumption which only an academician would attempt. Nevertheless, the attempt is here being made just as the problems of Japan's future have to be discussed and decided upon by responsible officials within the United Nations.

It is not the purpose of this volume to present either official or definitive answers to the many and detailed questions of Japan's future. This book has been written in the hope that it will aid Americans in forming their own opinions on the postwar treatment of our defeated enemy. The author expects wide disagreement with many of his conclusions, but by thus stimulating public thinking and discussion on a problem of vital concern to all Americans, the purpose of the book will have been served.

In preparing this study the author has had the advantage of participation in three study groups on the subject of Japan conducted under the auspices of The Institute of Pacific Relations in Washington, D. C., during 1943-4. Results of similar discussions held by various groups in China and Great Britain have been examined as have the reports of discussions conducted by the Universities Committee on Postwar International Problems in the United States. The author wishes to acknowledge the opportunity provided by the Canadian Institute of International Affairs in June and July 1944 to give a series of lectures across Canada on this subject, which enabled him not only to test his ideas but to obtain opinions from representative Canadian groups and to sample American

West Coast opinion on the treatment of Japan. The author had the further advantage of attending the Ninth Conference of The Institute of Pacific Relations in January 1945, where the problem of Japan was discussed in four round tables with representatives of twelve countries having interests in the Pacific area.

The American Council, Institute of Pacific Relations, kindly provided a grant-in-aid to the author for research during the summer of 1944, which is gratefully acknowledged. The author is further indebted to members of the staff of both the American Council and International Secretariat, I.P.R., for suggestions and criticisms while the manuscript was in progress.

This volume appears under the auspices of the American Council, Institute of Pacific Relations. The material that it contains relates closely to the general research program on problems of the Pacific Area being conducted by the Institute. The purpose of this series is to relate unofficial scholarship to the problems arising from the present conflict in the Far East with a view to indicating the major issues that must be considered in any future adjustment of international relations in this area.

Needless to say neither the American Council, the International Secretariat, or The Institute of Pacific Relations as a whole assumes any responsibility for statements of fact or opinion in this book. For all statements of fact and opinion the author cheerfully accepts the sole responsibility.

W. C. J.

Washington, D. C.
April 1945

Contents

THE FUTURE OF JAPAN

I

The Problem of Japan

A DEFEATED and disarmed Japan cannot be written off as a weak and unimportant nation in the Far East after this war. The future of a nation of seventy million people, which has ranked as a great power for the past fifty years, is a problem of vital concern to all the United Nations. The policies and actions of the United Nations toward a defeated Japan will primarily determine whether the Japanese can develop a stake in peaceful relations with their neighbors, or whether they will be consumed with efforts to revenge their defeat in a new outburst of aggression at the first opportunity. Determining these policies and actions will be no easy task.

In dealing with a defeated Japan we are handicapped by the false impressions we received in the past, deliberately created by the Japanese to check our opposition to their aggression. We underestimated Japan's strength and purpose. We overestimated Japan's progress toward popular government and the establishment of peaceful relations with other nations.

The course of Japanese aggression has been marked by the largely successful efforts of Japanese propagandists to make us believe that population pressure, lack of natural resources, and barriers to their trade were the primary causes for Japanese expansion, instead of justifications for their ambition to dominate the Far East. We were lulled into a false sense of security by Japanese who told us that each aggression was their last and that Japan had no intention of menacing our interests or risking war against the democracies. We were misled into regarding Japanese politics simply a struggle between war-minded 'militarists' and peace-minded civilians. We were assured that the 'moderate' or 'liberal' Japanese needed only time to check the ambitions of the 'militarists' and that any interference with militarists' actions from the outside would only consolidate their power within the nation.

Fundamentally, we, and all peoples who have been the object of Japan's expanding conquests, failed to understand that behind Japan's thin veneer of modernism was a nation that had not discarded the ideas and structure of an autocratic, militaristic feudalism. Such a nation, having obtained the weapons of modern power, must inevitably menace its weaker neighbors and ultimately threaten the security of all nations. We failed to appreciate this fact, primarily because, having admitted Japan to an international community that was attempting to establish principles of good faith and fair dealing among its members, we wishfully believed that the Japanese were capable of accepting these principles and acting upon them.

If we are to be successful in preventing future Japanese aggression and assisting Japan eventually to become trustworthy by our standards, we must try to understand the Japanese as they are, not, as in the past, we hoped they had become.

Japan is, in fact, a unique nation—a nation with a modern exterior and feudal insides. Within Japan, the Imperial Throne symbolizes the 'superiority' of a people descended from the gods and divinely destined to greatness and power. The Emperor is the incarnation of the nation's founding dieties and the 'father' of the Japanese people, to whom supreme loyalty is the subject's highest duty. Japan's 'modern' government is a structure within which the nation's real rulers—militarists, business men, politicians, and bureaucrats—unite in varying combinations to control the national destinies and bend the people to their will. Japan's economy is dominated by the wealthy few, who have monopolized the fruits of modern industry and denied them to the masses. Japanese society is a rigid system in which conformity to custom and tradition is tenaciously extolled by a people who have long been taught by the ruling oligarchy that poverty is a virtue, scarcity is an asset, and frugality and spartan living are matters of national pride. This is the real Japan that lies behind the façade of modernism.

In dealing with a defeated Japan we are also handicapped by the lack of previous experience. For unlike Germany, Japan has never lost a war. There is no record of a Far Eastern 'Versailles' to guide us or to indicate the past mistakes we must seek to avoid. We are not dealing with a counterpart of Hitler and his Nazis. But we are dealing with a nation in which Nazi ideas of racism, cultural superiority, and world domination have been part of the fabric of a feudal society in existence for centuries and little changed by the impact of western civilization. We are not dealing with an Asiatic counterpart of the Italian constitutional monarchy, perverted and subdued by a black-shirt leader and his gang. But we are dealing with an Imperial System—a line of emperors 'unbroken for ages eternal'—supported by myths and traditions that have provided an ideal base for modern militarism and aggression.

The United Nations must be prepared to deal with a defeated Japan as but a single part, if the principal one, of a total Far Eastern peace settlement. For the first time since the continental conquests of Genghis and Kublai Khan in the thirteenth and fourteenth centuries, war has come to the whole of Asia. There is hardly a corner of Asia or the Pacific area untouched by the direct or indirect effects of this war. Japan's initial conquests and her ultimate defeat will thoroughly scramble and upset patterns of international relations and national life that were centuries in the making. A whole system of colonial rule has been thrown into turmoil. A new Philippine Republic, a Korea to become independent in due course, together with Thailand, will increase the number of small nations across the Pacific. It is certain that the people of India will refuse to accept a return to their pre-war status. The bonds by which the western nations held China in subservience to their commerce, their finance, and their politics have been severed. Japan's defeat will remove the one Asiatic nation ranked among the great powers, and a revitalized Russia will assume a new role in the Far East and may struggle with China for leadership in Asia.

Most important of all is the fact that the primary pattern of East-West relations will not survive this war. This was a pattern developed during three centuries of expanding imperialism, which brought almost the whole of Asia and the Pacific area under the influence and domination of western nations. It was a system of relations between governments and between individuals characterized by paternalism and superiority on the part of the white man toward the peoples of Asia. The strength and quality of oriental civilizations were ignored by white men, who regarded the darker-skinned inhabitants of Asia as heathens, and by western governments, which regarded Asiatic territory as a fair field for exploitation and a golden opportunity to increase the wealth, prestige, and power of their nations. The white man possessed the superior skills and superior force that enabled him to place most of Asia under bondage.

These bonds have been broken and they can never be successfully repaired. They were broken by Japan—an Asiatic nation—at Shanghai, at Hongkong, at Pearl Harbor, at Manila and Singapore, at Rangoon and Batavia. They were broken because Japan—an Asiatic nation—dared to challenge the West in the one field where the white men had actually been superior, the use of force. It will matter very little to the peoples of Asia that this challenge of Japan met defeat. They will not soon forget the rapidity with which the flag of the rising sun was raised over the strongholds of western power in Asia. And they know the cost, in time and effort, that has been necessary for the western nations to bring about Japan's final defeat.

Long before Japan struck, many of the people of Asia had begun to believe that the much-vaunted white man's superiority was a myth, that it was not due to an inherent difference caused by the color of skin, but only to a difference in degree of opportunity, education, and learning. They had become convinced that the white man possessed no monopoly on modern skills, techniques of organization, and operations of government. In all countries of Asia a few set out to prove their beliefs. But progress was slow because the white man did possess a monopoly of power. It was this power that Japan so successfully challenged, gradually at first in China after 1931, and spectacularly throughout Asia after Pearl Harbor. Japan's initial successes will not be wiped out in the minds of the peoples of Asia, no matter how crushing her ultimate defeat. For what Japan once did, she or other oriental nations can do again and perhaps with more permanent success.

A defeated Japan cannot be dealt with in a vacuum, any more than can Germany. Disarmament of Japan must be coordinated with the organization of a United Nations security system and ultimately with a system of armament regulation for all nations. Establishment of economic controls to prevent Japan's rearmament will have a direct effect upon the broader questions of trade, tariff policies, and access to raw materials. Disposition of the territory occupied by Japan, partially determined at Cairo in 1943 by the leaders of China, Britain, and the United States, will raise other territorial questions, such as the status of Hongkong, the future of the mandated islands in the Pacific, and the position of the colonies in southeast Asia. The type of political regime in Japan that receives support from the United Nations may create precedents respecting the recognition of political regimes in Thailand, Korea, and other areas.

Formulating policies toward a defeated Japan and carrying them out successfully will constitute a major test of the willingness and the ability of the United Nations to work together in constructing a peaceful world, just as they have fought together in winning a world war. There should be no illusion that prevention of future Japanese aggression or prevention of any aggression in Asia and the Pacific can be guaranteed by the action of any one nation or by any special combination of nations that excludes others with a direct stake in the maintenance of peace in the Far East. It must be the common effort of the United Nations.

The broad objectives of United Nations policy toward Japan have already been outlined by official declarations and by statements of United Nations leaders. We start with the declared aim of total defeat for Japan, now assured by the progress of the war. A disarmed Japan, kept disarmed so that it will be unable to commit aggression in the future, is the second aim. A reformed Japan, peaceful and trustworthy, is the ultimate goal of United Nations policy.

These three objectives are the framework within which a host of decisions must be made. These decisions cannot await Japan's final surrender. Japanese reactions to defeat must be estimated and policies formulated to take account of possibilities ranging from last-ditch resistance to revolutionary chaos or sudden surrender. Policies will have to be formulated with respect to the restrictive measures applied to Japan, which will include disarmament, demobilization, discrediting the militarists, trial and punishment of war criminals, reparations, and the establishment of controls to prevent Japanese rearmament. The purpose, extent, and duration of United Nations occupation of Japan must be carefully considered, since actions taken during the period of occupation may vitally affect the course of Japan's postwar political, economic, and social development.

The growth of a peaceful and trustworthy Japan, eventually worthy of full membership in the international community, is contingent on United Nations agreement on more positive measures of assistance to the Japanese in undertaking the fundamental reforms necessary to peaceful development. Such measures will relate to the future position of the Imperial Throne and to the reconstruction of the political, economic, and social institutions of the country.

For Americans, the future of Japan is a special problem. This is true not only because the United States, as the greatest power in the Pacific, has a responsibility for leadership in the peace settlement, but also because the long history of conflicting policies between Japan and the United States has made the Japanese regard America as their number-one enemy. An unreformed Japan is certain to be a menace to the general peace and security as well as a specific threat to the United States. American leadership can do much to insure the development of a reformed and peaceful Japan in the future and thus contribute to the security of all nations.

II

Reactions to Defeat

How will the masses of the Japanese react when, for the first time, the remnants of their beaten army and navy return to a homeland that itself has felt the enemy's bombs? Will defeat change the attitude of the people or the position of the politicians, the bureaucrats, the business men, and the militarists who have controlled the nation? Will defeat alter the status of the Emperor? Will it bring about violent revolution led by liberals or by extreme militarists? No final answers can be given to these questions, but some of the probable effects of defeat can be charted in terms of our knowledge of Japan's history and present structure.

The end of the war will find the mass of the Japanese people tired—tired from long working hours, tired because of improper diet and lack of necessary medical care, tired of conforming to all the numerous restrictions and regulations of wartime government. A sharp break in the country's morale is bound to occur when Japan's leaders are unable to appeal for continued sacrifice in their 'sacred war.' Final surrender, however, will not produce an immediate change of heart among the Japanese. It will not induce a sudden love for democracy or a will to peace.

Final defeat will most likely produce the same psychological reactions in the mass of the Japanese population as have been observable in national crises in the past. Defeat will cause the traditionally minded Japanese to seek emotional outlets, not in a violent breaking with the past, but in a retreat to the past. Many Japanese may end their lives in a gesture of self-immolation or as an act of loyalty to their Emperor-father. Many will seek a haven for their disturbing thoughts in a more intensive contemplation of the glories of their ancestors and in that mystical nationalism which will permit them to accept the notion that this is not a lost war, but a temporary setback in their 'hundred-year' struggle to bring 'peace' to the world. Many Japanese will find satisfaction in the idea that defeat came because other nations failed to 'understand' Japan's 'unique' civilization and her 'true' aims. They will channel their emotions in an intense hatred of America and Britain, whose 'inordinate ambition to deny the right of existence to Japan forced the empire into this horrible war of unprecedented magnitude.' Many Japanese will derive emotional satisfaction through expressing sympathy for their fellow Asiatics of the 'co-prosperity sphere' who have been so unjustly denied the 'fruits' of Japan's victory just when they were beginning to understand Japan's 'benevolence' and appreciate the advantages of her 'leadership.'

Beyond these psychological reactions, however, the average Japanese will be concerned primarily with the struggle to make a living—a struggle that the war has made increasingly difficult and that peace may make even more intense. Concern over food, shelter, clothing, and a job will be uppermost in the minds of millions who have never known a high standard of living and to whom the Four Freedoms have no meaning.

It will not be surprising if the Japanese people appear child-like in their reactions and almost wholly bewildered, for through long years of war they have been denied access to knowledge about the outside world. They do not know what other people think about their nation's aggression. They do not even know the crimes their militarists have committed. Thanks to their war leaders, they have not had the benefit of world news-reporting, radio forums, or free discussions.

How will Japan's bosses—the bankers, big business men, politicians, bureaucrats, and the militarists—take defeat? They will be better prepared, for they will have foreknowledge of the end. Members of these groups are Japan's real rulers and war government has enabled them to strengthen their hold over the life of the nation. They will not want to see defeat wipe this out for their stake in Japan after defeat will be in maintenance of their power.

Leaders of these ruling groups, whether civilian or military, know full well that any protracted violence or any revolutionary activity in Japan as a result of defeat might bring such an upheaval in the political, economic, and social life of the country as to destroy forever their position as the final arbiters of Japan's destiny. In the past they have fought skilfully and courageously to maintain their power. They not only have the most to lose by violent upheaval but they also stand to gain the least by thoroughgoing reform. They are too intelligent to find satisfaction in an emotional retreat from reality or to martyr themselves by death. There may be some question whether Japanese armies will fight to the last man, but there is little question that Japan's ruling classes will use every stratagem to keep their power.

It is quite possible, therefore, that when the ruling groups are certain of Japan's military defeat, they will prepare to accept whatever terms the United Nations propose by organizing a cabinet designed to carry Japan through defeat into the postwar period with as little disturbance as possible to their own positions of power. Such a cabinet would most likely be composed of men known to have 'moderate' or pro-American or pro-British sympathies in the past. But it is inconceivable that any elements within these ruling groups would be parties to a proposal for greatly modifying or eliminating the Imperial Throne, upon which they depend for their authority.

In estimating the reaction of the Japanese to their first total defeat, the possibility of widespread civil disorder or violent revolution cannot be ruled out. There have been revolts in Japan's past history, but none in modern times that gained any significant mass following, or that was sufficiently strong or well-organized to oust the entrenched economic, political, and military rulers of the Japanese state. There have been no popular revolutions in modern Japan. There have been rice riots, strikes, and open conflicts of workers against employers and of tenants against landlords. Most often, however, these have been the attempts of small and relatively unorganized groups to redress personal grievances, to protest long hours and poor working conditions, or to express dissatisfaction with poverty-stricken conditions on the farm.

It is possible that defeat will produce similar civil unrest and outbreaks of violence. Then we may see many Japanese take advantage of a temporary breakdown of law and order to vent their grievances against war profiteers, greedy landlords, or rapacious local officials. But this kind of civil disorder, no matter how widespread, is not revolution. Revolution involves organized violence for specific purposes, which would be possible in Japan only under certain conditions.

There would have to be an almost complete breakdown of government authority and maintenance of order, at least in the industrialized sections of Honshu and Kyushu, for some period of time. For revolutionary groups will have little chance to strike successfully so long as adequate policing can be maintained under the authority of even the prefectural and municipal governments. A revolution directed at upsetting all or part of Japan's rigidly controlled society can be broken by the police with the aid of the patriotic societies and their gangs of ruffians who have been used to suppress liberal ideas, 'dangerous thoughts,' labor movements, and popular dissatisfaction since the beginning of the Meiji period in 1868.

Given the necessary disruption of governmental authority and police power, a successful revolution would depend upon the strength of revolutionary groups and upon leaders willing and able to risk their lives and seize authority. Scattered uprisings would have to be channeled quickly into organized activity if any revolution is to succeed and not collapse through lack of motive power.

Are there groups of any consequence or any men of recognized ability who might spearhead a liberal or popular revolution against Japan's war-lords and ruling classes? We know that for more than a decade prior to Pearl Harbor Japanese authorities were purging communists, labor and agrarian leaders, and others accused of espousing 'dangerous thoughts.' The official *Japan Year Book* for 1940-41 records over 60,000 arrests for the previous ten-year period. These arrests have continued since Pearl Harbor and the result has been to drive liberals and radicals underground, with the consequent weakening of organized activity. There is little information available concerning the composition, strength, aims, or influence of liberal and radical groups in Japan at present, and not much can be learned about them until final surrender breaks the rigid police controls and the 'thought' suppression so long maintained.

The whereabouts, activities, and influence of such recognized liberals as Toyohiko Kagawa and Professor Tatsukichi Minobe are unknown. In fact, most Japanese who had gained a reputation as protagonists of liberal political and economic ideas before the war are now well advanced in age and it is doubtful whether they will have the energy to exert much leadership if they survive the end of the war. That these 'elder liberals' still possess some standing and influence, however, is evidenced by the fact that in June 1944 the Japanese Supreme Court was reported to have acquitted eighty-two-year-old Yukio Ozaki of a charge of disloyalty to the Emperor. One of the few liberal statesmen still in public life, Ozaki has served both as Minister of Justice and Minister of Education in Japanese cabinets and has been a member of the House of Representatives since 1890. He was charged with disloyalty to the Emperor for criticizing the government's war policy in speeches supporting the candidacy of another liberal, Daikichiro Tagawa, for a seat in the House. That Ozaki apparently has a large following is indicated by his continuous re-election to the House and by the fact that he was re-elected in 1942 by a substantial vote at the time he was under the accusation of disloyalty. Tagawa, whom he supported, was not elected, but did receive a considerable vote, although little else is known of his influence.

It is quite possible that the most vigorous leadership in any popular revolution against the old Japanese ruling groups may come from among those Japanese prisoners of war who have been receiving indoctrination and training in Free China. With the assistance of the Chinese, two Japanese leaders who escaped from Japan have been conducting schools for these war prisoners. One school has been conducted near Chung-king by Wataru Kaji, a Japanese left-wing writer of some reputation in his own country, and the other is operating in Yenan under the direction of Susuma Okano, a leading Japanese Communist, with the assistance of the Chinese Communists.

Kaji is one of the founders of the Japanese Anti-War League and was employed by the Chinese Government to conduct a school for selected Japanese war prisoners, with a view to their use as propagandists against Japanese soldiers in China. The Japanese prisoners are given facts about the causes for Japan's war on China and are told how the militarists have dominated their country's policies to the detriment of the people. They are treated well so that when their minds are rid of the idea that captured Japanese soldiers are killed and tortured, they can be used at the front lines to urge Japanese troops to surrender. Those who successfully pass their indoctrination are not only used for propaganda work at the front but also as interpreters and for intelligence work.

In Yenan, a more comprehensive program of training and indoctrination has been carried out under Okano's direction. His school has been in operation for several years and he has organized the Japanese People's Emancipation League among the Japanese prisoners of war captured by the Chinese Communists. The object of this League and of part of the indoctrination given at his school is to train Japanese who will go back to Japan after the war and work for a program of agrarian and political reform. Okano's position as an outstanding Japanese Communist made possible the assistance of the Chinese Communists and their willingness to give him virtually a free hand in running his school. War prisoners who have successfully passed through the school are used for both propaganda and intelligence work by the Chinese Communist forces at the front and in the guerilla areas. It has been reported that some 600 Japanese war prisoners have received training at this school and, since they come mostly from peasant families in Japan, many of them may become leaders of popular movements within their respective communities when they return.

That opposition to Japanese militarism and dissatisfaction with the totalitarian system still exists among the Japanese is supported by the fact that a Japanese Communist leader was able to join Okano in Yenan in 1944. He escaped after long imprisonment and was aided in making his way from Japan through Korea and Manchuria to the Chinese Communist areas by Japanese sympathizers.

It is possible that if Japan's final defeat necessitates invasion of her home islands and is accompanied by a breakdown of Japanese government, popular pressures, long dammed up within the country, may burst all bounds and many of the old political, economic, and social ideas and institutions will be swept away. It is likely that leadership of any liberal or popular revolution in Japan after defeat will come from Japanese little known in the West and from groups brought together by the exigencies of war.

In any event, the forces that would be aligned against a popular revolution in Japan are so formidable as to indicate that one could only succeed with the active support of the United Nations. Yet such support, in the eyes of the Japanese, might label its leaders 'quislings' or 'collaborators' with Japan's enemies and thus nullify their chance of achieving a mass following. Regardless of this risk, however, United Nations refusal to support a popular revolution in Japan might result in destroying the most promising, although possibly weak, vehicle for the ultimate elimination of her militarism and excessive nationalism. Agreement among the United Nations on which leaders and which groups to support, and what steps, possibly including force, are necessary to effective support of a liberal revolution are major problems that will be considered in subsequent chapters on occupation and on political reconstruction.

Given a general breakdown of law and order, a more likely revolt would be one led by a combination of Japan's numerous and well-known ardent militarists and super-patriots. These most extreme nationalist leaders might stage a *coup d'état*, blaming the loss of the war on a home-front failure, not a front-line defeat. Bureaucrats, business men, and politicians, together with the more cautious militarists, could be made the victims of those extremists who have always believed in direct action. There would probably be numerous assassinations and an attempt to seize the Capital and the organs of government. Mass welfare would be their announced objective, but their methods would be those of fascism and totalitarianism.

Such a revolution was foreshadowed in the abortive army 'revolt' of February 1936, when a band of young army officers and men from the ranks attempted the assassination of seven of Japan's highest officials, including the Prime Minister. General Watanabe, Inspector-General of Military Education, Finance Minister Takahashi, and Admiral Viscount Saito, Lord Keeper of the Privy Seal, were killed but the remainder escaped. The 'rebels,' numbering about 1500, seized control of a central area in Tokyo, which included the Houses of Parliament, the residence of the Prime Minister, the War Office, and the Metropolitan Police Office. The manifesto they issued reads in part:

The essence of the Japanese nation consists in the fact that the Emperor reigns from time immemorial down to the remotest future in order that the national glory may be propagated over the world so that all men under the sun may enjoy their lives to the fullest extent . . . Now is the time to bring about an expansion of the power and prestige of Japan.

. . . many persons have made their chief purpose in life . . . amassment of wealth regardless of the general welfare and prosperity of the people . . . the majesty of the Empire has been impaired . . . Elder Statesmen . . . financial magnates, government officials . . . political parties are responsible . . . Japan now confronts a crisis . . . it is our duty to take proper steps to safeguard our fatherland by killing those responsible. On the eve of our departure for Manchuria we have risen in revolt to attain our aims by direct action. We think it is our duty as subjects of His Majesty the Emperor.

Allowing for the fact that translation into English cannot fully convey the Japanese meaning, the purport of the manifesto is clear. It represented a growing feeling among Japan's extreme nationalists that the modern political system of their country was rotten, that it gave power and wealth to the few who thus were able to withhold the profits of empire from the many. The solution of these rebel elements was not to take power from Japan's economic and political overlords and give it to the many. Their aim was a militarist dictatorship on the national-socialist model.

This kind of revolt is a possibility either before or after total defeat, because its chances for success are much greater than those of a popular revolution. Mass support could be gained by using all the old nationalistic slogans. It could be gained by the assertion, already made many times in the past, that the 'moderates,' through their retention of constitutional government, parliament, and parties, had perverted the Japanese Government to western ideas in disobedience to the injunctions of the 'divine ancestors' and against the 'true' advancement of Japan's 'Imperial Way.'

The potential leaders of a military *coup d'état* are numerous, influential, and experienced. In the army itself, in the reservists' associations, the patriotic groups, and the secret societies, these leaders possess strong organizations that could be mobilized for action with members already skilled in murder, torture, and terroristic activities. They would gain support from the demobilized soldiers and sailors to whom defeat will mean not only loss of a job and loss of sustenance but also loss of honor. They would have little opposition from the people, who have long been trained to obey their superiors and to regard the military as especially favored, since they act directly under the Emperor. They would have the natural opposition of the ruling bureaucrats, politicians, and business men, whom they would displace in power if successful. But even among this opposition, there would be many far less fearful of a revolution designed to preserve and

expand a totalitarian system than of one that aimed to overthrow it in favor of popular government. These civilians
would either cast their lot with the extreme militarists in hope
of some future gain for themselves, or would fade from sight
temporarily, knowing that ultimately they would be called
upon to help run the government.

Seizure of power in Japan by the militarists would mean
the preservation and intensification of all the ideas and institutions that have furnished the motive power for Japanese
aggression in the past. If successful, it would place in power
the very groups most likely to sabotage disarmament and
most likely to begin undercover preparations for another war.
For these reasons alone, if such a militarist revolt comes after
surrender, it must be crushed by the United Nations, by force
if necessary, for it would be the worst possible beginning for
the construction of a peaceful Japan.

The way in which the Japanese take defeat, therefore, will
be an important factor in all United Nations measures
adopted to disarm the nation, keep it disarmed, and aid it
toward a peaceful future. Because it is not possible to predict
Japanese reactions with any exactness, the United Nations
must be prepared beforehand to deal with any number of
possibilities; but however the Japanese react, the United Nations can still stand firm in a determination to insure against
future Japanese aggression and to support those Japanese who
desire to make their defeat a starting point for reform and not
a revival of reaction.

III

Surrender and Occupation

No matter how the Japanese react to defeat their unconditional surrender is to be required and Japan is to be occupied. Unconditional surrender of all Axis powers was agreed upon at the Casablanca conference in January 1943, and at a press conference the reports of which appeared on August 19, 1944, President Roosevelt, following a discussion of plans for the occupation of Germany, stated that it should be as easy to reach agreement with China on the occupation of Japan and that he and Generalissimo Chiang Kai-shek had already discussed the matter.

It is possible that there will be no general surrender by Japan's military authorities and government, if they decide to prolong the war by widespread guerilla resistance. This might mean that acceptance of the terms of surrender by the Japanese would be delayed until order was restored and some Japanese government was recognized by the United Nations. Aside from this possibility, unconditional surrender will be offered by the Japanese at the point when they have become convinced their cause is lost and further resistance is of no value. In either case, the United Nations must decide who shall be required to agree to the terms of surrender. These terms may be extensive and include all matters relating to Japan's postwar status, or they may only include the immediate requirements for disarmament and demobilization, leaving to a treaty of peace or future agreements the detailed obligations to be imposed upon Japan for purposes of preventing a renewal of aggression.

Past practice dictates that the terms of surrender must be agreed to by the chiefs of staff heading the armed forces of the defeated nation. This assumes that their orders to cease hostilities will be obeyed by all of their subordinate commanders. It also assumes agreement to the terms of surrender by the head of the state. It does not always mean agreement by the government in power, since the necessity of surrender may have caused the government's dissolution.

The United Nations desire not only unconditional surrender by Japan but also recognition by the Japanese people of their total military defeat, so that they may hesitate again to embark on war. In view of this dual objective, the terms of surrender should be agreed to by all those Japanese most responsible for waging the war. These would include:

1. The Emperor, who is Commander-in-Chief of all the armed forces and who alone has the final constitutional power to wage war and to make peace

2. All members of the General Staffs

3. All military and naval officers who hold or who have held cabinet posts during the war

4. All members of any existing cabinet at the time of surrender

5. The ex-prime ministers who have taken the place of the *Genro* or Elder Statesmen as advisers to the Emperor and who have been used by Premiers Tojo and Koiso as an advisory group for the conduct of the war.[1] Requiring the Emperor and this large group of Japanese leaders to sign the terms of surrender need not prejudice future decisions of the

[1] The living premiers, with the dates of their incumbency are: Baron Reijiro Wakatsuki (April–December 1931), Admiral Keisuke Okada (July 1934–March 1936), Koki Hirota (March 1936–February 1937), Baron Kiichiro Hiranuma (January 1939–August 1939), General Nobuyuki Abe (August 1939–January 1940), Admiral Mitsumasa Yonai (January–July 1940), Prince Fumimaro Konoye (June 1937–January 1939; July 1940–July 1941; July–October 1941), and General Hideki Tojo (October 1941–August 1943).

United Nations on such questions as the retention of the Imperial Throne or recognition of any particular Japanese government either during or after occupation.

To repeat, the immediate purposes of this proposal would be, first, to force the highest Japanese officials to agree to the terms of surrender so that lesser Japanese officials would enforce these terms, and second, to show the Japanese people that total defeat is a fact acknowledged by their Emperor and his highest officials. Accompanied by widespread publicity, the accomplishment of these purposes might be the first step in discrediting militarism and in convincing the people that aggression does not pay.

The nature, extent, and duration of United Nations occupation of Japan will be partly determined by military necessities and partly by whether occupation is to be undertaken for other than military reasons. A Japanese government may accept unconditional surrender before all its armies have been beaten in the field and before its homeland has suffered extensive destruction. Or it is possible that the Japanese may not give up until the bulk of their armies have been destroyed, their navy immobilized, and their home islands considerably devastated and even invaded by the United Nations. And there is the final possibility that total defeat will require the crushing of numerous centers of resistance both inside and outside of Japan, with no general surrender taking place. Military necessity—what it takes to bring about complete surrender by the Japanese—will be the first determinant of the extent and number of forces required for the occupation of Japan.

Widespread destruction of industries and of Japan's centers of population may necessitate extensive occupation by military forces and the employment of a large number of civil-affairs officers in order to carry out immediate tasks of relief, including the restoration of public services, transport, control of disease, and distribution of food and clothing among a bombed-out population. Again widespread destruction plus actual hostilities within Japan may so disrupt Japanese life and the functioning of Japan's government as to require extensive occupation, the establishment of Allied Military Government, and the use of large United Nations forces to restore and maintain order. Finally, and regardless of the requirements above, occupation with the use of sizable contingents of United Nations troops, at least in the beginning, will be necessary to bring about the disarmament of Japan and the demobilization of her armed forces.

Future events will define the military purposes of occupation and partly determine its extent and duration. But our experience in Europe suggests that while the exact situation in a country cannot be foretold, it does not do to improvise policies on the spot. Estimates must be made of probable conditions to be met, and alternative policies must be devised concerning both military and other purposes of occupation.

It must be decided, before occupation begins, whether one of its purposes shall be the maintenance or restoration of law and order, regardless of the internal consequences for the Japanese, or whether, if any mass uprisings occur, such activity will not be interfered with so long as it is directed against the 'militarists and warmongers.' In his New Year's message on January 1, 1944, Generalissimo Chiang Kai-shek asserted that President Roosevelt had agreed with him that 'if the Japanese people should rise in revolution to punish their warmongers and overthrow their militarist government, we should respect their spontaneous will and allow them to choose their own form of government.' The question whether the United Nations will permit the Japanese to adopt a militarist-fascist regime seems to have been answered by President Roosevelt on February 12, 1943, when he said,

No nation in all the world that is free to make a choice is going to set itself up under a Fascist form of government, or a Nazi form of government, or a Japanese war-lord form of government. Such forms are the offsprings of seizure of power followed by the abridgement of freedom . . . Therefore, the United Nations can properly say to these forms of government two simple words: 'Never again.' The right of self-determination included in the Atlantic Charter does not carry with it the right of any government to commit wholesale murder or the right to make slaves of its own people or of any other people in the world.

The maintenance of law and order in Japan could be a relatively easy or an extremely difficult task for the occupation forces, depending upon the extent of civil strife and the strength of any revolutionary outbreaks. If violence should occur on a sizable scale as a result of the organized efforts of any group or groups attempting to seize control of the government, United Nations authorities in charge of the occupation forces would be confronted with very delicate decisions. They would have to determine whether this violence represented a real effort on behalf of the common people against their militarists and toward a more democratic government, or whether it was merely the attempt of another clique trying to gain power for its own selfish ends. This might easily involve United Nations forces in action supporting violence by some groups while suppressing violence by others.

Again, it must be decided whether occupation of Japan is to be used for the purpose of impressing the Japanese people with the fact of their defeat. This has been termed a 'token' or 'symbolic' occupation and has been widely advocated in the United States and other countries. Military considerations aside, this would involve occupation of most key cities and towns in Japan so that few Japanese would be ignorant of the

presence of foreign troops on their soil. It would not necessarily mean the use of very large forces or have to be of long
duration.

It is very important in the case of Japan that the forces
used for occupation, no matter for what purpose, be representative of all of the United Nations engaged in the struggle
against Japan. This is necessary not only to impress the Japanese with the unity of the nations arrayed against their aggression, but also to prevent them from asserting that occupation
is an act of racial discrimination, the effort of the white race
to dominate an Asiatic nation. For this reason, it would be
highly desirable to include forces from China, the Philippines,
and from other parts of the 'co-prosperity sphere' liberated
from Japanese control. Dividing Japan into zones to be occupied by forces of the different major powers (the plan to
be applied to Germany according to the Crimea Declaration
of February 11, 1945) would seem unwise in view of constant Japanese attempts to define the war against them as an
imperialist effort of Great Britain and the United States. Occupation zones might be used for purposes of a centralized
command and administration, but forces representing all of
the United Nations fighting Japan should be distributed in
all zones. The establishment of a Central Control Commission
for Japan, similar to that contemplated for Germany in the
Crimea Declaration, would be a valuable means of co-ordi-
nating the policies and actions of the United Nations during
the period of occupation.

Finally, the most controversial of all policies to be decided
upon is whether occupation of Japan is to be used, beyond
the requirements of military necessity and disarmament, for
the purpose of initiating those fundamental political, economic, and social reforms deemed necessary for the development of a peaceful Japan. Acceptance of this policy would
involve careful planning, considerable preparation, and a large

and well-trained staff for its execution. It would also involve deciding whether occupation and administration of Japan should be continued until the United Nations are convinced that the tasks of reform can be safely entrusted to the Japanese or, whether the United Nations should limit the period of occupation, undertaking only those reforms which could be brought about immediately and which would have some chance of becoming permanent when occupation forces were withdrawn.

The idea of taking advantage of occupation for the purpose of bringing about reforms has met with strong objections. Attempts at enforced reforms are held to be unworkable, with little chance of success. To impose any alien ideas or institutions on the Japanese, it is asserted, would not only stiffen their desire for revenge and increase their hatred of the United Nations, but would also violate the United Nations principle of self-determination. Occupation for this purpose has also been opposed on more practical grounds. In an article in *Harper's Magazine* for April 1944, Nathaniel Peffer asserts that there are not enough persons trained in Japanese language and customs or skilled in public administration to staff a long-term occupation government for Japan. The only extensive training program for occupation administration is that being conducted in the United States for army and navy officers. Although the number of men trained in this program is considerable, the purpose of the training is limited to producing civil-affairs officers who can administer invaded areas to prevent interference with military operations from behind the lines. However, these officers could be used in administration of Japan after final surrender if broader objectives for such administration are fully agreed upon and planned.

From other United Nations come still different objections to the proposal of occupation and administration for the purpose of reforming Japanese ideas and institutions. A British

group states that 'There could be no surer way of playing
into the hands of the military caste, discredited by defeat,
than to corral the people of Japan in an Anglo-Saxon kinder-
garten of internationalism.' Chinese, Filipinos, and representatives of other Asiatic peoples have objected to occupation for
reform as too closely resembling the old pattern of western
imperialism, by which Japan might tend to become a new de-
pendency of the western nations.

The duration, extent, and purpose of United Nations occupation of Japan will depend upon many military and non-
military considerations, some of which cannot be properly
assessed until final surrender is obtained. Experience gained
in United Nations occupation of Germany should prove a
valuable guide to policies subsequently adopted for Japan.
But no matter how far the United Nations are willing finally
to go in an attempt to initiate reforms in Japan's political, economic, and social systems, the general policy adopted for
occupation of Germany and announced at the end of the
Crimea Conference could be applied equally to Japan as a
minimum basis for United Nations occupation policies. To
demonstrate this, that part of the Crimea Declaration relating
to Germany is reproduced below with the words 'Japan,'
'Japanese,' and 'Japanese militarism' substituted for 'German,'
'Germany,' 'Nazi,' and 'Nazi militarism.'

It is our inflexible purpose to destroy *Japanese* militarism and
to insure that *Japan* will never again be able to disturb the peace
of the world. We are determined to disarm and disband all *Japanese* armed forces; break up for all time the *Japanese* general
staff that has repeatedly contrived the resurgence of *Japanese*
militarism; remove or destroy all *Japanese* military equipment;
eliminate or control all *Japanese* industry that could be used for
military production; bring all war criminals to just and swift
punishment and exact reparation in kind for the destruction
wrought by the *Japanese*, wipe out the *Japanese militarists*, their

laws, organizations and institutions, remove all . . . militarist influences from public office and from the cultural and economic life of the *Japanese* people; and take in harmony such other measures in *Japan* as may be necessary to the future peace and safety of the world. It is not our purpose to destroy the people of *Japan*, but only when *autocracy* and militarism have been extirpated will there be hope for a decent life for *Japanese*, and a place for them in the comity of nations.[1]

Whatever measures are undertaken during the occupation of Japan for the purpose of preventing future Japanese aggression, there is one governing factor which must constantly be kept in mind, that unless the Japanese are able to undertake the reforms by which the people can obtain the instruments of popular control over their government and the means of achieving economic security for themselves, the obstacles to the growth of a peaceful Japan will still remain. Reform in Japan will be harder to achieve than in Germany, for the Japanese have never had any experience in democracy. United Nations policies, therefore, must take into account all the obstacles to reform in Japan during the period of initial occupation of the country, when actions taken or not taken may have a decisive effect on the trend of Japan's postwar development. Some such principles as the following are proposed as essential:

1. Occupation should be undertaken to whatever extent necessary to bring about the complete defeat and final surrender of the Japanese.

2. Occupation should be undertaken to the extent and for the period necessary efficiently to disarm the Japanese and demobilize their armed forces.

3. Regardless of military necessities, limited forces, representative of all the United Nations engaged in the war against

[1] Italics indicate substitutions.

Japan, should be stationed for a brief period in all key cities and towns, to symbolize Japan's defeat.

4. United Nations occupation authorities should suppress, by force if necessary, any attempt by militarist groups to seize control of the government.

5. If a liberal revolution directed at the ousting of Japan's old ruling coalition should occur before or during occupation, the United Nations should either (a) take any necessary steps in its support, including use of force to suppress its opponents, or (b) maintain law and order and prevent violence from any source while at the same time providing full opportunity for liberal groups to be heard, to appeal to the people, and to obtain control of the government by lawful processes.

6. During the period of occupation, the United Nations should initiate directly and/or support the initiation of those minimum and essential reforms—political, economic, and social—necessary to the development of a peaceful Japan. The duration of occupation for this purpose alone should not be prolonged beyond the point where there seems to be a reasonable chance that the Japanese can carry forward these reforms by themselves. (See Chapters IX, X, and XI, for more extended discussion of these reforms.)

7. The preceding principle involves acceptance by the United Nations of a responsibility to assist the Japanese in the continued reformation of their national life once occupation has ended.

IV

Disarmament

DISARMAMENT of Japan is the agreed aim of the United Nations. In his message to Congress on January 7, 1943, President Roosevelt stated:

It is clear to us that if Germany and Italy and Japan—or any one of them—remain armed at the end of this war or are permitted to rearm, they will again and inevitably embark upon an ambitious career of world conquest. They must be disarmed and kept disarmed . . .

Minimum measures to disarm Japan include geographic disarmament, or the elimination of Japanese control over conquered territory useful for strategic purposes or as a source of war materials; the destruction or disposal of existing Japanese armaments after hostilities have ended; and the destruction or reconversion of war plants and industrial facilities. There is also involved the demobilization of all Japanese armed forces and the dissolution of militarist organizations and patriotic groups, measures treated in the following chapter.

A modern nation's war power rests upon the proper combination of many complex factors. Large-scale industrial development, adequate supplies of raw materials, and skilled technicians and workers can be used to produce the whole range of weapons needed for modern war. A large population can provide the reservoir of man-power necessary to large armed forces. Control of strategic territory can secure a nation's defense and furnish bases for offensive operations. Deficiencies in raw materials can be partially remedied by conquest of areas where these resources are found.

In her home islands, Japan possessed a large and growing population from which to draw the man-power for her armed forces and the skilled technicians and workers for her industry. Originally with foreign aid, the Japanese gradually developed an industrial system capable of producing all of the weapons of war. Japan's attempt to develop her war power, however, was handicapped at the start by her lack of many strategic raw materials and by her vulnerable geographic position close to the Asiatic continent. The Japanese perceived these deficiencies quite clearly and set out to remedy them.

A series of piecemeal conquests in less than half a century materially enhanced Japan's war-making power to a point where her war-lords were willing to take the final risk of war against their most powerful opponents, America and Britain. Each conquest improved Japan's strategic position and provided a springboard for new conquest. Each conquest gave Japan control of new supplies of raw materials. Acquisition of the Liuchiu archipelago and the Kurile Islands in the 1870's aided the fishing industry, thus increasing Japan's food resources, and gave her defense points in the Pacific to the north and to the south. Annexation of Korea provided more food resources, a new labor supply, and valuable gold and timber reserves. Korea was a stepping stone to Manchuria. Expansion into Manchuria enabled the Japanese to exploit large resources of coal and iron and to build an industrial base that made possible conquest in China south of the Great Wall. Acquisition of Formosa early in the game and of the German islands in the Pacific in 1919—the Marshalls, the Carolines, and the Marianas—extended Japan's footholds far to the south, forming a protective screen for her rapid conquests of the Philippines and the countries of southeast Asia in the present war.

Elimination of Japanese control over the conquered territories that so materially increased their war-making power was the subject of the first official United Nations declaration concerning the future of Japan after defeat. At the end of the Cairo Conference, held in late November 1943, Generalissimo Chiang Kai-shek, Prime Minister Churchill, and President Roosevelt issued a joint communiqué, which stated that the three great allies were in agreement

that Japan shall be stripped of all the islands in the Pacific which she has seized or occupied since the beginning of the first World War in 1914, and that all the territories that Japan has stolen from the Chinese, such as Manchuria, Formosa and the Pescadores, shall be restored to the Republic of China. Japan will also be expelled from all other territories she has taken by violence and greed. The aforesaid three great powers, mindful of the enslavement of the people of Korea, are determined that in due course Korea shall become free and independent.

This agreement disposes of most of the territories conquered by Japan since 1895. The first reference to 'islands in the Pacific' presumably is to the Marshall, Caroline, and Marianas groups mandated to Japan under the League of Nations after 1919. On the continent, the return of Manchuria to China would imply return to Chinese control of the provinces of Jehol and Charhar and the remaining sections of Inner Mongolia occupied by Japan between 1933 and 1938. The territories from which Japan is to be 'expelled' obviously refer to her southern conquests—Indo-China, Malaya, Thailand, Burma, the Netherlands East Indies, and the Philippines. Although the Cairo declaration allayed fears regarding the future disposition of certain areas, such as Manchuria and Korea, and announced the intention to reduce Japan ter-

ritorially as a measure of disarmament, it did not directly indicate what was to be done with other areas acquired by
Japan at different times since 1870. Because of their strategic
importance, the status and possible disposition of these areas
will bear examination.

The Liuchiu archipelago links Japan's southernmost island
of Kyushu with Formosa. Long before Japan was opened to
the West, the inhabitants of these islands were paying tribute
to both Japan and China. In the 1870's a dispute arose between Japan and China over the harsh treatment of Liuchiu
fishermen by Formosan savages. When negotiations failed to
satisfy Japan in 1874, a Japanese punitive expedition was dispatched to Formosa, but the Chinese asserted their sovereignty over the Formosans and dispatched troops for their
protection. Negotiations were again resumed, during which
the Chinese acknowledged that the Liuchiu islands were a
part of Japan. A formal Chinese recognition of Japanese sovereignty over the Liuchiu archipelago was given in 1881.
Japan's acquisition of these islands was as much due to laxity
on the part of China as to her own ambitions, for the Chinese
could have asserted claims to them equally as valid as the
Japanese. Nevertheless, their acquisition, judged in the light
of Japan's internal politics, was part of a growing desire for
conquest by the Japanese, and it partially satisfied some of
Japan's budding imperialists at home who at the time were
urging a move into Korea, a move which other Japanese felt
was premature.

The strategic location of the Liuchiu islands enclosing the
East China sea and screening the China coast makes their control by Japan in the future a danger to Chinese security. Since
Japan acquired the islands as the result of threats and might
be said to have taken them because of 'greed,' they could be
given to China as the nation which once had claim to ownership. If this disposition should not be considered desirable,

then these islands, together with the Bonin and Volcano groups, should be brought within whatever scheme is established for the former Japanese mandated islands.

The Bonin islands and the smaller and neighboring Volcano islands were annexed by Japan in 1876 and 1891 respectively.[1] These two island groups guard the southern approaches to Japan and are about 700 miles from Tokyo. Their strategic significance has been dramatized by the furious and bloody battle for Iwo Jima, one of the Volcano group. About 500 miles east of the Bonins and approximately 1200 miles from Tokyo is Marcus island, a lone outpost of Japanese defense. In any postwar security system designed to prevent future Japanese aggression, control of these island groups would seem necessary to provide easy access to Japan. While not taken by 'violence,' although possibly by 'greed,' their usefulness to the United Nations for security purposes would be ample reason for eliminating Japanese control over them.

To the north of Japan lies Sakhalin island, slightly larger than Formosa and geographically a northward extension of the main Japanese group. Japan obtained control of the southern half of Sakhalin by the Treaty of Portsmouth following her successful war with Russia in 1905, just as Formosa was obtained from China by the Treaty of Shimonoseki following the war with China in 1895. To restore the southern half of Sakhalin island to the Soviet Union would be as logical as restoring Formosa to China. The Soviet Union was not represented at Cairo because of her non-participation in the Far Eastern part of the war, so it may be presumed that disposition of this territory will be left for settlement when the Soviet Union makes its desires known. Transfer of the south-

---

[1] The Bonins were claimed for the United States by Commodore Perry after his first visit to Japan in 1853. This claim was never officially recognized by the American government.

ern half of Sakhalin to the Soviet Union would be a logical part of Japan's geographic disarmament and make the strategic position of Vladivostok more secure.

East of Sakhalin, and stretching from the northern Japanese island of Hokkaido to the southern tip of Russia's Kamchatka peninsula, are the Kurile islands which enclose the sea of Okhotsk. Japan's possession of these islands by occupation was confirmed by Russia in 1878. Even if ousted from southern Sakhalin island, through her possession of the Kuriles Japan could control the approaches to eastern Siberia, and it was the Japanese bases and weather stations on Paramushiro and some of the northernmost Kuriles which enabled her to plan the invasion of the Aleutian islands in the present war.

It can be argued that since the Kurile islands were not acquired by 'violence' and perhaps not by 'greed,' and were certainly not 'stolen from the Chinese,' Japan should not lose them. The seizure of a part of Japanese territory as a punitive act would only serve to inflame the hatred of the Japanese toward the United Nations and particularly toward the Soviet Union and the United States, the obvious strategic beneficiaries of such action. On the other hand, if geographic disarmament is to be imposed upon Japan at all, it should be carried out thoroughly, and except as bases for the fishing industry these islands have a far greater strategic than economic value to the Japanese. In his radio address from the Puget Sound Navy Yard upon his return from the Aleutians, President Roosevelt emphasized the importance of strong American bases in Alaska and the Aleutians after this war, for American defense. The Kuriles stand in the same relationship to Japan as do the Aleutians to the United States, and they could be taken from Japan at the time of surrender as a measure of geographic disarmament. Since possession of these islands by either the Soviet Union or the United States could be objected to on many grounds, joint control or control by a United Nations agency, in which Canada, China, the Soviet Union, and the United States are represented (and ultimately, Japan) would seem preferable. Japan might be permitted exclusive use of the islands for her fishing industry and the exclusive right to exploit any resources found in them. Common use by the United Nations of weather-reporting services in the islands would be important both in relation to the development of air transport across the northwest Pacific and for weather forecasting in Canada and the United States. A disarmed Japan would have no need for the exclusive use of these weather stations. If this proposal is rejected and Japan is permitted to retain the Kuriles, all Japanese military and naval installations in the islands should be destroyed and all weather-reporting services operated by the Japanese should be made freely available to other nations.

Complete geographic disarmament, then, should include the elimination of Japanese control over those island groups not mentioned by the Cairo Declaration—the Liuchiu archipelago, the Bonin and Volcano islands, Marcus island, the southern half of Sakhalin island, and the Kuriles. Stripped of these territories plus those covered by the Cairo Declaration, Japan would be reduced to her home islands, an area of approximately 145,000 square miles. This was the territory held by Japan when she started her career of conquest as a modern nation after 1853.

Unconditional surrender will compel the Japanese to turn over to the United Nations all armaments still in their possession—guns, munitions, planes, naval vessels, tanks, and all other kinds of movable military equipment. The only question here is whether all these armaments shall be destroyed or how they shall otherwise be disposed of. Much of this equipment will be captured in the course of hostilities, but considerable armaments may be left intact in Japan or elsewhere when surrender comes. It is possible that the Chinese or Filipinos or other people in the 'co-prosperity sphere' may desire to seize Japanese equipment remaining in their territories as partial compensation for war damages. If captured intact, trucks and other types of vehicles would probably be useful and those not useful in whole or in part could be salvaged as scrap. Movable armaments in Japan would either have to be destroyed or otherwise removed from Japanese control. It will make little difference how such materials and equipment are disposed of so long as the Japanese are deprived of their use.

Naval vessels will probably be the most important items of Japan's armament for disposal after the war. Chinese sources have indicated that China expects some proportion of whatever Japanese navy is afloat after hostilities and the Filipinos and the Dutch may also wish to benefit in this manner. Probably the most sought-after ships will be the cruisers, destroyers, and smaller armed vessels which could serve China or other nations as coast-defense ships, useful in patrol work and anti-smuggling operations. Neither China nor any other Asiatic nation would find it economical or desirable to acquire the heavier battleships or aircraft carriers.

Fixed or immovable armaments will also have to be destroyed or removed from Japanese control. These will include coastal-defense batteries, anti-aircraft installations, army and navy bases, training camps and barracks. Such defenses and installations remaining in Japan can be easily found and broken up or otherwise rendered useless. Those remaining in other areas retaken from the Japanese can be destroyed or handed over to the legitimate government of the territory.

It will probably be impossible, as well as a waste of time, for United Nations agents to attempt the seizure and destruction of all small arms and small stocks or supplies and ammunition. These items can be easily hidden and their possession by the Japanese has no significance in terms of disarmament or future aggression. There is one item of equipment, however, which some experts suggest should be removed from Japanese possession as a psychological measure: that is the Japanese sword.

From ancient times the sword has been the symbol of valor and of the martial arts in Japan. It was the prized possession of the old *samurai* or warrior class in feudal Japan and has continued to be the most valued piece of military equipment for Japan's modern militarists who have inherited the *samurai* traditions. One of the three sacred treasures of Imperial Japan, in custody of the Emperor, is the sacred sword, said to have been found by the sun-goddess, Amaterasu-Omikami, in the tail of a dragon. The art of sword making was highly developed in ancient Japan and has been continued in modern times. Large sums have been spent on fine examples of the sword-makers art, and loss of his sword by an officer can bring great dishonor upon him.

Because of the importance of the sword as a visible symbol of militarism, it has been proposed that all Japanese possessing swords handed down in their families be required to give them up as token of the final obliteration of the militarist spirit of the nation. While there is much to be said for such a proposal in terms of its psychological effect, its enforcement would be extremely difficult, because of the ease with which a sword can be concealed. Such an act, too, having no real military significance in the physical sense, might have the opposite of the desired result and cause the Japanese to become even more desirous of revenge against an act they would regard as one of sheer barbarity by foreign officials.

Disarmament must also include destruction or reconversion of manufacturing facilities producing weapons, munitions, and all of the large and small items needed for a complex war machine. It is essential that Japan's war plants and machinery be reconverted for production of non-war materials or if that is impossible, as might be the case with certain special machinery, such items must be destroyed. If reports from Japan are correct, so widespread has been the conversion of Japan's industrial system to war purposes that peace-time products have been reduced to the minimum essentials. It was reported in 1944, for example, that almost the whole textile industry was being converted to making of munitions and airplane parts. Here is a phase of disarmament that relates directly to Japan's future. To insist that the Japanese immediately reconvert their war plants to the manufacture of non-war products without providing them an opportunity to plan their postwar production might retard the whole process of disarmament. It would not contribute to an economically healthy Japan in the future, but rather deepen the hatred of the Japanese against the victors. So long as the process of reconversion is supervised by the United Nations and no war materials are being produced, there seems to be no reason for hastening the process and good reason for relating it to Japanese plans for development of their postwar economy.

The geographic disarmament of Japan and the elimination of Japanese possession of movable and immovable armaments will probably be the easiest measures undertaken by the United Nations against Japan after defeat, for they will involve little controversy and their execution will not be complicated. The requisites of this disarmament can be summarized as follows:

1. All territories outside of Japan's main islands acquired since 1870 should be removed from Japanese control.

2. All armaments in Japanese possession at the end of hostilities should be destroyed or removed from Japanese control.

3. All war plants, facilities, and tools used in the production of armaments should be destroyed or converted for peace-time use.

4. Consideration should be given to requiring the Japanese to give up their swords as a symbol of defeat and of the end of Japanese militarism.

5. Consideration should be given to permitting the Japanese to convert their war plants and facilities to peace-time production gradually and in relation to their new economic policies, with adequate United Nations inspection to insure against continued production of armaments or munitions of any kind.

V

Demobilization

THE measures of disarmament outlined in the previous chapter can severely reduce Japan's material resources for war, but they will not reduce her human resources for war-making. Demobilization must accompany disarmament as a guarantee against future militarism and aggression. Initial steps in this process must include demobilization of Japan's armed forces, dissolution of militarist organizations, trial and punishment of war criminals, and discrediting the militarists in the eyes of the Japanese people.

Should the Japanese be permitted to retain any portion of their armed forces? Experience with German disarmament after the last war provides the answer to this question. Germany was permitted to retain an army of one hundred thousand men, for maintenance of internal order, which was made the nucleus for Hitler's *Wehrmacht* under the leadership of professional army officers who planned and sought revenge in another war. To permit Japan's militarists the same opportunity would be to risk nullifying all other measures of disarmament, for Japan's armed forces have been the base of mass support for Japan's militarism and conquest.

Under the Japanese conscription system, the army is drawn chiefly from the farmers and other low-income groups in the population. This mass of the people are literate but vastly ignorant of the ideas, customs, and psychology of other nations. They have always been receptive to the slogans and appeals of the militarists concerning Japan's 'uniqueness' and her 'divine' mission to dominate other peoples. When the soldier finishes his term of service, he brings to his family and neighbors all the ideas of excessive nationalism and imperialism he has learned in the army. He is encouraged to retain and to spread these beliefs through the propaganda activities of the reservist associations and the various patriotic societies. The navy requires better educated men on the whole, but although reputed to be less extreme in their beliefs than the soldiers, many sailors have been no less fanatical in support of armed conquest. All military personnel receive similar chauvinistic indoctrination.

The members of Japan's armed forces have been the link between her militarist leaders and the people providing an easy means for dissemination of their propaganda. To leave Japan with any organized army or navy would be to leave the militarists who planned this war a perfect instrument for maintaining their prestige and influence among the people and for fomenting a spirit of revenge for another series of conquests.

The main case for leaving Japan any military establishment is that her postwar government may need military forces, in addition to local police, to maintain law and order and to retain its authority. However, if the Japanese domestic police forces prove unable to maintain law and order in the country during the period of occupation, the United Nations must assume responsibility for doing so, and if it is believed that a Japanese government may have difficulty in maintaining order after the bulk of United Nations forces have been withdrawn, the United Nations should undertake to organize and train a more adequate domestic police force before the end of the period of occupation. A reorganized police force would be desirable in any event, because in the past the regular police have too often been identified with the secret police (*Tokkoka*) of the Home Ministry and the gendarmerie (*Kempeitai*) of the War Office in the suppression of civil rights and of liberal and democratic movements. Abolition of the secret police and of the gendarmerie is essential, and together with the reorganization of the Japanese police would be a major measure toward demilitarizing the nation.

When hostilities are ended, the United Nations presumably will have a large number of Japan's armed forces under their control as prisoners of war. As prisoners, they will have been disarmed and will be under guard in camps in many of the territories formerly occupied by Japan, as well as in Japan itself. The question is whether the United Nations will simply repatriate troops held abroad as quickly as transportation permits and release those held in Japan as soon as hostilities are over, or whether the whole process of demobilization will be planned and supervised in relation to conditions in Japan and to other policies of occupation and disarmament.

Planned demobilization involves several considerations. First, if there is turmoil and chaos in the country as a result of defeat, it would seem undesirable immediately to return Japan's beaten forces to their homeland and at once to release troops held within Japan. Released soldiers and sailors would only constitute one more disturbing element and a threat to the restoration and maintenance of order. Second, the process of disarmament might well be completed before the military forces are permitted to return to civilian life. This would prevent sabotage of disarmament by those groups most likely to interfere with an action they can hardly accept without rancor. Third, the ability of the Japanese to channel these men into civilian life without a sudden disruption of the labor market would be greatly facilitated by United Nations collaboration in planning and supervising demobilization of the armed forces. The timing and method of demobilizing Japan's military personnel will vitally affect the orderly fulfilment of the terms of surrender and the rapid accomplishment of Japan's disarmament.

Demobilization of the Japanese army and navy will contribute to the demilitarization of Japan, but the ideology of militarism will not disappear unless those militarist and patriotic organizations which have been so closely interwoven with its development are dissolved. They must be dissolved as a part of the process of disarmament and demobilization.

Foremost among these groups are those openly militarist in character. The largest of this type is the Ex-Service Men's Association or *Teikoku Zaigo Gunjinkai*. Organized in 1910, it is said to have a membership of over three million, with branches in all parts of the country. This association, together with the semi-official Young Men's Associations, has served as most effective means of perpetuating and intensifying the myths and beliefs of emperor-divinity, extreme nationalism, and imperial expansion. Similarly, the *Dai Nippon Butoku Kai*, a sports association organized in 1906, with a membership of over two and a half million, has for its purpose 'the encouragement of the martial arts.' For army officers the *Kaikosha* or Military Club was established in 1877 to 'cultivate the spirit of patriotism.' Its membership is reported to be more than twice as large as the *Suikosha* or Naval Club, which had a member list of 11,700 in 1937 and was founded in 1876 for the same purpose as that of the Military Club. Built around these frankly militarist societies are numerous smaller organizations for encouragement of study and research in subjects closely related to military matters, such as aeronautics, radio, weather reporting, and allied subjects. These societies have always received the encouragement of the militarists and super-patriots and constitute a direct medium for their propaganda.

But almost equally important have been the so-called 'secret' societies and patriotic groups, which have been much written about in recent years. These are generally small in membership but since the beginning of the Meiji period have possessed power and influence far out of proportion to their size. Some have been primarily propaganda agencies, while others such as the *Kokuryukai*, or Black Dragon Society, have included thugs, assassination squads, and bullies to terrorize officials deemed 'weak' or 'unpatriotic' by their leaders. Mitsuru Toyama, the leader of the Black Dragon Society who died in October 1944 at the age of 90, was sometimes called the 'unofficial emperor' because of his power and immunity from any prosecution for the assassinations and terrorist activities which he directed.

The *Genyosha*, or Dark Ocean Society, was the forerunner of these groups. It was formed in 1881 by a merger of three groups stimulated by the activities of Takamori Saigo, the 'hero' of all Japanese super-patriots, whose exploits have become legendary. The *Genyosha* and the *Kokuryukai* still exist and, together with such extreme nationalist societies as the *Dai Nihon Seinenkai* and the *Dai Nihon Saisanto*, would form a natural rallying point for embittered militarists and patriots if permitted to continue their activities after the war.

The organizations mentioned in the foregoing paragraphs are but examples of many existing militarist and nationalist societies. Their activities and leaders have been succinctly characterized by a student of Japanese political history as follows: [1]

Their chiefs have played a role in Japan similar to that of the Rosenbergs, Goebels, Heines, von Killingers and Streichers in Germany. It should not be forgotten that for decades these societies have had a virtual license to poison the minds of the Japanese people by the crudest chauvinism and by propaganda supporting aggression; they have been permitted to terrorize liberal and intellectual leaders, or anyone speaking in favor of friendly relations with the outside world. They have organized gangs of terrorists in China and Manchuria, specializing in murder, opium-

[1] 'A Canadian View,' *Pacific Affairs*, June 1944, pp. 195-6.

selling and prostitution; they have served as an unofficial espionage service for the Japanese army, particularly in Asia. In short,
they have acted at once as the spearhead of Japanese aggression
both in mass propaganda and espionage; their continued activity
should be completely frustrated.

The enforced dissolution of all Japanese militarist organizations and patriotic societies by the United Nations is just as
important as the dissolution of the Nazi Party in Germany
and the eradication of Nazi organizations. Dissolution of
these Japanese societies is equally important as a measure of
disarmament and a necessary corollary to demobilization of
Japan's armed forces.[1] The Japanese must not be forced to
lay down their arms and still be permitted to carry on their
propaganda for aggression and their training for war through
civilian organizations.

The trial and punishment of Japanese accused of war
crimes is already being planned by the United Nations and
this measure early received the attention of United Nations
officials. On October 7, 1942, President Roosevelt reminded
the country that crimes against the civilian populations of the
areas occupied by the Axis nations were still continuing, and
he declared it to be 'the intention of this Government that
the successful close of the war shall include provision for surrender to the United Nations of war criminals.' He stated
that the United States was prepared to co-operate with other
United Nations in establishing a United Nations Commission
for Investigation of War Crimes. Such a Commission was
subsequently organized, and on June 29, 1943, in announcing
the appointment of an American representative on this Commission, President Roosevelt stated,

It is hoped that the Commission, which will have its headquarters in London, will be able to take concrete steps looking to the

[1] See next chapter for discussion of enforcement.

punishment of agents of the Axis powers who have perpetuated atrocious crimes against their innocent victims.

Until recently the work of this Commission has been concerned almost wholly with preparations for the trial and punishment of German war criminals. But it is clear that this United Nations policy applies to Japan as well as to Germany. It is known that lists of Japanese who may be charged with war crimes are being compiled in the United States and in other member countries of the United Nations. In March 1944, China established a War Crimes Commission, headed by Dr. C. T. Wang, former Ambassador to the United States, which has since announced that it is at work and is ready to receive evidence of Japanese war crimes. In November 1944, it was announced that a sub-committee for the Far East and the Pacific of the United Nations War Crimes Commission had been set up in Chungking to prepare for the eventual trial of Japanese war criminals and to correlate information and evidence submitted by individual nations. A special committee for this purpose has also been established under the Adjutant-General's Office of the United States War Department.

Presumably, Japanese accused of war crimes will be tried in the area in which the crime was committed, by regular or by specially constituted national courts. This would apply to crimes committed outside of Japan, since it is probable that within Japan, war criminals will be tried by a United Nations tribunal. It is likely that most Japanese accused of war crimes will be members of the armed forces or of the secret police and gendarmerie.

It is certain, however, that any method of trial and punishment for specific crimes will leave unscathed a considerable number of Japanese whose responsibility for the war and for Japan's policy of aggression may be far greater than many of those brought to trial. The acts of terrorism and atrocities committed by the Japanese have been the end-products of these war-makers' policies. It has been suggested, therefore, that some attempt be made to bring to trial those Japanese, whether militarists or civilians, who have been chiefly responsible for supporting and permitting the acts of terrorism and assassination, both at home and abroad, which have aided Japan's policies of conquest. It is contended that it should be possible to find the Japanese guilty of such acts—unqualifiedly crimes—under Japanese criminal law, or if this is not possible, they might be convicted of treason or political crimes against the state. It is believed that these men are generally known and that their responsibility can be established. Many Japanese might be found who would furnish evidence against them, once the power of the militarists and their henchmen has been broken.

Whatever policy is followed in bringing to trial Japanese accused of war crimes, it would be highly desirable to apply the same general principles with respect to Japanese as it has been decided to apply to the Germans. Likewise, it is desirable that the whole procedure of trial and punishment be carried through with the minimum delay, as nothing could contribute more toward fostering a revengeful spirit than long-drawn-out trials of war criminals.

Surrender and demobilization will not automatically cause the militarists to lose their traditional prestige, nor will disbandment of militarist and patriotic societies. Too many Japanese in the armed forces will escape punishment for war crimes. With their prestige intact, they could become the nucleus for a revival of military power—a group subversive of democracy, liberalism, or reform, experienced in political manipulation and mass propaganda, and inevitably bound to seek revenge in another war. The existence of such a group would constitute a major barrier to the rise of new and more liberal leaders.

Japan's militarists have already laid the basis for preserving their prestige by a home propaganda launched in the summer of 1944, which explained that Japanese defeats in the Pacific were due to the superior weapons and equipment of their enemies, but asserted that Japan's spirit was still indomitable. Continuing this 'line' after defeat, the militarists could claim that Japanese honor was not crushed, Japanese skill and intelligence did not fail, but only the lack of adequate weapons caused the Japanese to cease fighting. If the Japanese people could be persuaded to accept this propaganda, then they may be led to believe that, with their co-operation, deficiencies in weapons will be remedied in the future—and the militarists' prestige will have been preserved.

While some officers and men will undoubtedly find adequate or even lucrative employment in civilian pursuits, for many a return to civilian life will mean severe readjustments and they will be tempted to direct their efforts toward regaining a better position for themselves in the profession they know best—war-making. It is worth recalling that the forerunner of all super-nationalist societies, the *Genyosha*, was organized with the support of the *samurai* (pre-Perry militarists), who lost their means of employment when the feudal system was abolished in 1868. Dissatisfied with the small pensions they received and with government policies of the day, they became willing supporters of such super-patriots as Saigo and Toyama. With their leaders, they plotted methods of forcing the government into foreign wars and furnished the gangs of toughs who terrorized officials and ordinary citizens who were attempting for the first time to exercise what little rights they had under their new constitution.

To prevent a recurrence of this development and further

to destroy the influence of the militarists in Japan a number of proposals have been made to discredit this large group. Perhaps the most drastic suggestion is that all army officers of the rank of Lieutenant-Colonel and above, and all navy officers of the rank of Captain and above be exiled and interned outside of Japan for an indefinite period. This would apply to between six and twelve thousand men. They would have to be held outside of Japan in a large number of small camps, so that the solidarity of constant association of large groups would be broken, and they would have to be virtually cut off from all communication with Japanese at home. The length of their exile and internment would have to be regulated by Japan's political development after the war. The cost to the United Nations of a ten- or fifteen-year internment for this number of persons would be negligible compared to the cost of defeating Japan in another war.

A variation of the foregoing proposal is that all officers and men in the army and navy at the time of surrender be taken prisoners of war and interned for a brief period in this status. As prisoners they would be treated in strict accordance with the terms of the Geneva Convention, which has been followed during the war by the United Nations. It is suggested that the necessary prisoner-of-war camps be scattered through the Japanese main islands, so that the Japanese people would see their soldiers and sailors, and, more importantly, their officers, even the highest ranking ones, behind barbed wire as prisoners of the United Nations. On release they would return to their homes as civilians, stripped of their uniforms, insignia, and military privileges.

The principal objections to either of these proposals are, first, that it would make martyrs of the Japanese military so dealt with, in the eyes of their families and of the Japanese people, and thus raise rather than lower their prestige. Second, it is asserted that the roots of Japanese militarism are so traditional and psychological that it cannot be pre-determined by the United Nations whether any specific measures will diminish the intangible 'prestige' of the militarists. Since these proposals might produce the opposite of the desired result and enhance rather than discredit the prestige of the militarists, it would seem better to rely on the measures of disarmament, total demobilization, and dissolution of militarist and patriotic societies for discrediting the militarist groups.

Proposals relating to total demobilization of Japan's armed forces and their supporters can be summarized as follows:

1. All Japanese armed forces should be totally demobilized, the army and navy organizations abolished, and the War and Navy Departments in the government, along with the cabinet posts of War and Navy Ministers, eliminated.

2. Demobilization should be so controlled as to prevent any interference with the process of disarmament and to aid in the economic transition from war to peace.

3. The gendarmerie of the War Office and the secret police of the Home Office should be abolished. If necessary, the United Nations should assist in a reorganization and re-training of the domestic police forces so as to provide the Japanese government with a means of maintaining order. It might also be useful for the United Nations to insist that the police forces be under the direct control of local and provincial governments rather than completely under the Home Office, as in the past.

4. All militarist organizations and patriotic societies should be dissolved by public action of the Japanese government, and their revival in any form should be prohibited.

5. Japanese war criminals should be tried and punished in accordance with principles agreed upon by the United Nations and comparable as far as possible to procedures used in the trial and punishment of German war criminals.

VI

Reparations and Economic Controls

TOTAL defeat, unconditional surrender, disarmament, and de-mobilization are only part of the price Japan must pay for having embarked upon a course of aggression. There remains for consideration the question whether Japan shall pay reparations, and the problem of how best to prevent her from reacquiring the sinews of war in the future—the raw materials and the industrial machines necessary to equip armed forces for a new aggression.

The determination of the amount of money, goods, or services that Japan shall pay as reparations depends upon the *purpose* for which reparations are to be exacted, and the *capacity* of Japan to pay. Reparations could be exacted solely to reduce Japan's war-making power. They could be used to aid in rehabilitation and reconstruction of Asiatic areas devastated by hostilities. Or, they could be required primarily as a punitive measure further to demonstrate to the Japanese people that aggression must be paid for. Any one of these purposes or a combination of them must be considered in relation to the long-range goal that Japan become a 'peaceful nation,' possible only if she develops a healthy economy.

Japan's ability to provide reparation payments for any purpose will depend, among other factors, upon an estimate, after surrender, of the nation's productive capacity in terms of the actual destruction of her industrial plant and equipment and in relation to the peace-time consumption needs of her population. The fact that disarmament will relieve the Japanese from the burden of devoting a large proportion of

53

their industrial capacity to production of uneconomical armaments will be an additional and an important determinant of Japan's ability to provide reparations.

Experience gained by the Allied and Associated Powers of World War I with the problem of German reparations indicates that requiring a defeated enemy to pay a huge sum of money as reparations is both impractical and unwise. Similarly, experience in the last war demonstrates that payments in goods and services must be adjusted to the requirements of international trade and that reparations should be limited to fixed amounts to be paid within a fixed period of time. Bearing in mind the purposes of reparations, the factors affecting Japan's capacity to pay, and the experience of the last war, it is possible to consider the various forms of reparations payments that may be required of the Japanese.

Prior to Pearl Harbor, the United States, Great Britain, and the Netherlands 'froze' all Japanese assets and property in their respective territories. In the United States, it was estimated that the value of such assets and property seized was over $130,000,000. No estimates are available from Britain or the Netherlands. It has been proposed that all these assets be used to indemnify losses suffered by the nationals and governments of these three countries in the course of the war. What proportion of the total loss could be met by these Japanese assets cannot be determined until after the war, but it is known that the governments concerned have made a thorough investigation of all Japanese holdings, have established procedures for presentation of claims for damages by individuals, and are making estimates of damages to government property.

It is also proposed that Japanese property and assets found in reoccupied territories be seized as partial indemnification for war damages, by the government having sovereignty over such territory after the war. This would mean that the Chinese government would take over all Japanese assets and property found in occupied China, Manchuria, and Formosa. The Philippine Republic would do the same in the Philippine Islands. Japanese property in Korea would be taken over for benefit of the Koreans, and the same process would be followed in Indo-China, Thailand, Malaya, Burma, and the Netherlands East Indies. Each government would undertake its own arrangements for indemnification of its own citizens and subjects for war damages.

This proposal raises the question of whether property of private Japanese citizens should be seized, as well as that of Japanese government or semi-government agencies. It is contended by some that all Japanese business operations have become so inextricably involved with government financing and controls as to be inseparable from Japanese government property. It is the opinion of some Chinese, Filipinos, and Koreans, however, that any property that can be proved to have been wholly owned and operated by Japanese individuals or private companies before hostilities began should not be seized. It is doubtful whether this policy could be applied to more than purely personal holdings and small businesses when all the evidence is in, but this is an important aspect of reparations yet to be agreed upon by the United Nations.

The proposition that public and semi-public Japanese holdings in the former Japanese-controlled territory should be confiscated and used as partial compensation for war damages and as an aid to reconstruction seems generally acceptable. Industrial plants of all kinds, railways, warehouses, port installations, and public buildings would fall in this category. These enterprises have either been state-controlled or have been operated by state-controlled or semi-governmental corporations such as the South Manchurian Railway Company, the Manchurian Heavy Industries Corporation, the North China Development Company, and the

Central China Development Company with their numerous subsidiaries. Like corporations have been established for business operations in southeast Asia. Confiscation of the properties of these concerns would have the added advantage of eliminating Japanese economic interests outside of Japan—interests which have been vital to Japanese expansion in the past.

Another method by which the Japanese might be required to pay reparations is the production of commodities to be used in reconstruction of former Japanese-held territory as partial restitution for goods and properties destroyed in the course of the war. Japan could be required to produce such items as machine tools, light and heavy industrial equipment, chemicals, textiles, other industrial products, and consumers goods on a reparations account with the amounts fixed in terms of the needs of the recipient countries and a time limit set for their delivery. Such a plan would mean that the Japanese would have to supply the costs of labor and processing, but some arrangement would have to be made by which those raw materials not available in Japan's home islands and needed in production of the commodities required could be obtained. Since it would be impractical to require Japan to pay for these raw materials in gold and they could not be fully paid for in services, it has been suggested that the nations receiving such reparations in kind agree to supply Japan with the raw materials required in their production. The complexities of this plan with respect to the balance of payments and its effect on the revival of normal trade relations are such as to lead to the conclusion that reparations in goods would be feasible only if limited to those products Japan could manufacture with a minimum importation of raw materials, such as silk, chemicals, and light industrial equipment.

Still another method of reparations payments in kind would be to require Japan to transfer industrial plants and equipment to China and other areas that have suffered devastation in the war. Such a transfer probably would have to include the services of Japanese technicians to train operators of these plants and equipment, but they could be paid by the Japanese government as a part of its reparations account. This proposal has been advocated both as a means of weakening Japan's industrial power and as an aid to the industrial reconstruction of the former occupied territories. It would have to be considered as an alternative to the proposal that Japan produce goods in payment of reparations, since removal of any large amount of Japan's industrial establishment would preclude such production.

There are a number of disadvantages to this latter plan. Transfer of *heavy* industrial plants and equipment would not only present problems of transportation, but also would prove uneconomical from the standpoint of the recipient nations. It would be more profitable for China and other countries in Asia to build new heavy industries with the latest equipment than to accept plants from Japan, less modern and more expensive to operate. Furthermore, to remove any amount of heavy industry from Japan might only give the Japanese an opportunity to rebuild their industries with the latest improvements and modern equipment, thus giving her at once an important advantage over her former enemies and new competitors. While the transfer of *light* industries would be open to similar objections, such a transfer would be more feasible and perhaps of more advantage to the recipient countries. On the other hand, it would have the effect of preventing the Japanese from developing production of domestically needed consumer goods and would tend to force them to continue their former, internationally undesirable, policy of basing their economy on heavy industry and an expanding export trade.

The whole question of reparations in kind from Japan or of transfer of Japanese industrial plants to other parts of Asia may, of course, become an academic matter if the Japanese continue resistance within their home islands and prolonged air bombardment and extensive invasion are required to bring about their surrender. In this event, most of Japan's industries, public utilities, and transport system may be reduced to rubble, or so severely damaged as to require considerable time for reconstruction or replacement. Under any conditions the United Nations will have to co-ordinate their reparations policy with whatever economic controls are established to prevent rearmament and with the kind of economy the United Nations are willing to permit the Japanese to develop in the postwar world.

Final decisions on the question of reparations will probably be made with due consideration to China's demands, since the Chinese have suffered far more heavily than other nations at the hands of the Japanese. There have been Chinese advocates of all the proposals discussed above, but it is likely that when the Chinese agree among themselves, any reasonable proposal of theirs will be accepted by the United Nations. The previous discussion indicates that a reasonable plan of reparations for Japan should include fixed payments in goods (e.g. reparations in kind) within a specified time, with the amounts and kinds of commodities adjusted to the needs of the recipient countries. Specific reparations requirements should conform to the general policy that the purpose of reparations is neither to provide Japan inadvertently or otherwise with economic advantages over her neighbors nor to be so severe as to make Japan an object of international relief or a center of major economic instability.

Any economic restrictions or controls applied to Japan beyond reparations must be considered in relation to the prevention of rearmament and to the postwar economic position which the United Nations are willing for Japan to have. Two extreme points of view have been expressed concerning Japan's economic future. The opinion that Japan should be reduced to a 'pastoral nation' has been reported expressed by Rear Admiral Emory S. Land, Chairman of the U.S. Maritime Commission,[1] as well as by other Americans and Chinese in private discussions. This would involve reduction of Japanese industry to a bare minimum, forcing a far larger percentage of the population to depend upon agriculture for their existence. It has been proposed both as a measure of retribution for Japan's aggression and as a guarantee against future Japanese war-making. The opposite view is that postwar Japan be given equal access to raw materials with other nations and equal trade opportunities in world markets, without being made to suffer economic penalties and restrictions. This opinion is based on the assumption that Japan's aggression primarily resulted from her lack of resources and from barriers to her trade, and has been expressed by a number of Americans and representatives of American organizations often termed 'pacifist.'

Although Japan may in fact be reduced to a near-pastoral status before the war finally ends, as a result of widespread destruction, it is a reasonable assumption that the United Nations will not adopt either of the extreme policies described above. Japan will not be held down to a strictly agricultural existence or very soon given a free and equal position in world trade. Instead, there will be an attempt to set up those economic controls deemed most likely to prevent future Japanese acquisition of a war machine. Criteria for the establishment of such limited economic controls have been well stated

[1] Reported statement before a sub-committee of the House of Representatives' Committee on Postwar Economic Policy. *New York Times*, September 25, 1944.

by H. G. Moulton and L. Marlio in their study, *The Control of Germany and Japan:* [1]

First, the economic devices must not be permitted to throttle the economic life of the country against which they are imposed. It is an instinctive reaction to urge that aggressor nations should be crushed economically and kept permanently in a state of economic impotency. But, as realists, we are obliged to conclude that the solution is not so simple. Economic retrogression means chronic unemployment; chronic unemployment means perpetual social unrest and political tension; and this in turn fosters the spirit of revenge. Moreover, protracted economic depression in any important country inevitably has serious repercussions upon economic conditions in other countries . . . In an interdependent world we move forward, or backward, together.

Second, the economic control measures selected must be administratively feasible—relatively easy to enforce. A large army of foreign policing agents is a source of continuous humiliation and friction; hence the control measures should be of a character which require a relatively small number of controllers. For a similar reason the number of restrictive measures should be the minimum necessary to accomplish the essential objectives—therefore the greater the variety of control devices the greater the area of disagreement and friction.

The control of Japan's war-making power may prove to be less difficult than that of Germany's. Japan's power has been largely dependent upon control of non-Japanese territory containing essential war materials and essential strategic advantages against her opponents. Stripped of her empire, Japan's war potential will be greatly reduced, economic controls applied to her need not be extensive or complex, and enforcement of controls should be simpler in an insular country than in a continental one.

In terms of war essentials, Japan proper was relatively self-

[1] Harold G. Moulton and Louis Marlio. *The Control of Germany and Japan,* Washington, D. C., The Brookings Institution, 1944, p. 8.

sufficient only in the production of food, and was seriously deficient in most of the raw materials necessary for war purposes. Coal, copper, and wood pulp were the only materials of which Japan possessed a near sufficiency. Vital minerals including bauxite, nickel, lead, iron ores, tin, and zinc as well as crude rubber, petroleum, and cotton had to be imported from outside Japan proper in quantities ranging from 63 to 100 per cent of her total requirements. In preparation for war the Japanese had attempted to make up for these deficiencies to some degree by the development of chemical and metallurgical industries for the production of new materials and synthetics and by increasing their hydro-electric power output. The extent to which these efforts were successful in meeting Japanese deficiencies cannot be known until the war is over. But, regardless, it is safe to assume that given Japan's limited economic resources it will be possible to prevent her re-acquiring a war-machine by the control of a few essential items and key industries.

If Japan is reduced to her main islands, any future Japanese aggression must be an amphibious operation, and in such an action air power and sea power are the two main essentials. Therefore, elimination of Japan's air power coupled with a strict prohibition upon its revival in any form, and the reduction of Japan's merchant marine (her navy being eliminated as part of her disarmament) would seem to offer the two best means of preventing a reconstitution of her war-machine through economic controls. Even should she secretly acquire guns, tanks, and other munitions as well as an army, lack of an air force and lack of shipping to launch an overseas invasion would leave her vulnerable to attack and make conquest of adjacent territory virtually impossible.

To this end Japan should be prohibited from having any aircraft industry and any plants for the production of aluminum or magnesium, the light metals required in construction of planes. Japan lacks bauxite, alunite, and alumina, the basic minerals necessary to aluminum production. Although she also lacks any large deposits of magnesite, one of the minerals required for magnesium production, the Japanese have been experimenting with various modern methods of producing this light metal from chemical and mineral resources available in their home islands. A prohibition on Japanese imports of any of the raw materials required for aluminum production, and of magnesite would severely reduce the possibility that the Japanese could develop a light-metals industry. Japan's island position would make such import controls more easily enforceable than in the case of Germany, and regular inspections would ensure that the Japanese did not construct aluminum or magnesium plants or begin secretly to construct planes. In addition, the United Nations should exercise vigilance among themselves to see that the Japanese were not permitted to develop these industries in adjacent countries or to build planes and train an air force outside of their homeland.

Control over the aircraft industry alone would prevent Japan from obtaining the most essential weapon of modern war and make the Japanese vulnerable to air attack as a punitive measure by the United Nations in case these restrictions were violated. A more than adequate additional safeguard would be provided by control over Japan's merchant shipping.

It is apparent now that the Japanese underestimated their war shipping needs and that tonnage lost by submarine and air attack has been a major cause for the gradual contraction of their expanded empire. Prior to the war, Japan had increased her merchant tonnage to about 6,000,000, as compared to approximately 11,500,000 tons for the United States and over 21,000,000 tons for Great Britain. It has been estimated that of Japan's pre-war total, between 70 and 80 per cent had been sunk by January 1945.

Within the United Nations, there have already been proposals to prohibit or control Japan's retention of any merchant marine after the war and to sharply curtail or prohibit her shipbuilding industry. These proposals reflect a desire to weaken both Japan's military potential and her postwar competitive position in maritime trade. Specifically, it has been proposed that Japan would be permitted to build merchant ships, but that the total tonnage of ships built and operated by the Japanese should be limited to a fraction of her prewar shipping, something between the two and three million tons judged necessary for Japan's inter-island trade and a minimum share in Asiatic coast traffic. It has been further proposed that the size and speed of the merchant ships permitted Japan be limited and that former Japanese government subsidies to the shipping industry and operators should be prohibited. Such restrictions as these would have to be enforced through periodic inspections and some control over chartering of foreign ships by Japanese operators would have to be instituted.

A minimum disruption of Japan's economy would be involved in control over Japanese aircraft and shipping. A prohibition on all aircraft manufacturing, on aluminum and magnesium production, and on imports of the raw materials for these light metals would not seriously curtail Japan's productive capacity for peace-time consumer goods. The light-metals industries are relatively new to Japan and are in an experimental stage, so that substitutes for aluminum and magnesium can be developed without interference with established businesses. And finally, the small size of Japan's main islands makes air transport a luxury, not an economic necessity.

Control over Japanese shipping might work more of a

hardship, since shipping services have provided substantial income and also foreign exchange in countries abroad. The Japanese fishing industry has been an important element in the nation's economy by providing employment for over two million persons, by providing considerable food for the population, and through exports, providing a source of foreign exchange. The operations of the fishing industry extended to almost all parts of the Pacific along both the Asiatic coast and the coasts of North and South America. There will undoubtedly be a desire to curtail the operations of Japanese fishermen and whalers on the part of many of the nations around the Pacific after the war. However some Japanese fishing in the western and northern Pacific and perhaps southward will have to be allowed in order to give Japan opportunity to obtain sufficient fish for home-consumption needs. Restrictions might be established on the export of canned fish from Japan so as to reduce such wide-ranging operations of her fishing fleets as occurred before the war. Aside from the small ships needed for fishing, and a fair amount of merchant tonnage to handle Japanese inter-island shipping needs and a share in Asia's coastal trade, the bulk of Japanese foreign trade can be handled by foreign ships. So long as ocean freight rates remain equitable, this should not constitute too severe a limitation of Japan's postwar foreign trade.

In addition to controls over aircraft manufacturing and shipping, it has been proposed that all oil refineries and all plants for synthetic oil production be destroyed or converted to other uses, and that the Japanese be forced to import only refined petroleum products. This proposal is designed as an additional safeguard against development of an aviation industry and as a means of preventing the Japanese from stockpiling petroleum for potential war use. Enforcement of these restrictions would raise many difficulties and would offer many opportunities for evasion, since it would require a strict surveillance over Japanese imports of all petroleum products and an agreement on the part of the United Nations to regulate exports of these items to Japan. In addition, the task of determining whether the Japanese were exceeding their legitimate requirements for use of petroleum and were building up hidden reserves would require a large technical and inspecting staff within Japan.

From many persons in the United States and China have come proposals for more comprehensive control over Japanese economy than that contemplated in the measures discussed above. It has been proposed, for example, to limit or restrict the output of all Japanese industry, particularly iron and steel production, chemicals, and machinery, and to establish controls over Japanese imports of such strategic materials as iron ore, nickel, tin, lead, tungsten, and rubber. It is asserted that the experience of the United States, Great Britain, and other United Nations in the operation of import-export controls during this war has not only provided adequate experience and knowledge of methods to make such measures effective, but also has resulted in providing an adequate number of persons trained to operate such controls.

Widespread control of Japan's economy, as proposed above, has been objected to on the grounds that it would require too complex an organization and too large a staff to make enforcement effective. It is also asserted that such extensive control would tend to throw Japan's economy out of gear and consequently would necessitate continued economic assistance from the United Nations to avert a general Japanese economic collapse. Not only is doubt expressed as to the real effectiveness of such extensive economic controls, but it is asserted that, if employed, it would be much easier for the Japanese to show that the controls were damaging to the growth of a healthy economy and were preventing the introduction of needed economic reforms. The Japanese could blame United Nations restrictions for their own reluctance or failure to deal with their economic problems satisfactorily.

If reparations, economic restrictions, and controls are imposed upon Japan, it would seem desirable to confine them to those measures best calculated to prevent the re-building of a Japanese war-machine and least harmful to development of a healthy internal economy from which the Japanese people can obtain a greater benefit than they have in the past. With due regard for these qualifications, the following propositions are suggested with respect to reparations and economic controls:

1. All Japanese private business and government assets and property abroad should be confiscated as a part of reparations.

2. A fixed amount of commodities and materials (reparations in kind) should be required from Japan for use in reconstruction in former Japanese-occupied territories.

3. The amount and kind of reparations should be determined in relation to Japan's postwar productive capacity and with regard for the utilization of those products requiring a minimum importation of raw materials.

4. The period of reparations payments should be limited to not more than five years, with provisions that established schedules may be met ahead of time.

5. Japanese manufacture or purchase of airplanes, gliders, lighter-than-aircraft, airplane parts, and equipment should be prohibited.

6. Japanese ownership or operation of any international or domestic airlines should be prohibited.

7. Japanese production of aluminum and magnesium should be prohibited.

8. Japanese imports of aluminum, alunite, bauxite, magnesium, and magnesite ores should be prohibited.

9. Japan's merchant fleet should be limited to approximately 3,000,000 tons, and Japanese shipbuilding capacity should be restricted accordingly.

VII

The Problem of Enforcement

MEASURES for the disarmament of Japan and for the prevention of her rearmament have been discussed and evaluated. The United Nations must enforce these or similar measures until such time as they can agree to permit Japan the exercise of full rights, without restriction, in the international community. Agencies of enforcement must be agreed upon and procedures for applying penalties against Japan for violation of the terms of surrender must be established.

In preparing to deal with a defeated Germany, the United Nations set up the European Advisory Commission, which has provided the medium through which terms of surrender for Germany have been discussed, details of occupation worked out, and measures for Germany's disarmament and prevention of her rearmament have been devised. Officials of individual governments concerned are known to be at work on similar problems with respect to Japan, but it would seem equally necessary that the proposals of various governments be considered in an official body where common agreement can be reached on recommendations for final action by the United Nations.

The establishment of a Far Eastern counterpart of the European Advisory Commission would prove valuable, not only in dealing with Japan but also as a means of preparing for the settlement of many Far Eastern questions arising out of Japan's defeat. The initial task of a Far Eastern Advisory Commission would be to provide a means by which the official views of the United Nations could be brought together

68

and developed into a common agreement on the terms of surrender for Japan and on the establishment of enforcement
agencies and procedures. (As in the case of the European Advisory Commission, the resulting recommendations would derive from the pooling of ideas by official representatives of
the United Nations and a more thorough study of the advantages and disadvantages of proposed plans than is possible
through normal diplomatic interchange.)

The problems of enforcement of whatever terms of surrender are finally agreed upon for Japan are twofold. First,
there are the immediate tasks of enforcing disarmament, demobilization, and related actions, which must be carried out
as rapidly as possible after final surrender. Second, there are
the continuing tasks of preventing rearmament and enforcement of any controls set up for this purpose that must be
undertaken for as long as the United Nations deem necessary.

The immediate tasks of Japan's disarmament, the demobilization of her armed forces, the dissolution of reservist associations, militarist organizations, and patriotic societies, the
abolition of the secret police and gendarmarie, the trial and
punishment of war criminals, and any immediate measures to
discredit the militarists will be under the direction of the
military commanders in charge of United Nations occupation
forces. Removal or destruction of armaments existing in
Japan after defeat is not a difficult process. As has been stated,
it will do little good to carry this to the extreme of searching
out and destroying small arms and small stocks of ammunition, for these can easily be concealed, while tanks, planes,
heavy guns, naval ships, and fixed fortifications cannot. It is
important, however, that the process of disarmament be
closely supervised and carried out with a minimum of delay.
It will not do merely to require the Japanese to turn over all
movable armaments to the United Nations at a given time
and place and to destroy all fixed defenses by a given date,

for this places a premium on evasion. Under the Versailles Treaty, the Germans were given six months in which to deliver to the Allies the war materials they were to be deprived of as a part of their disarmament. When deliveries were not forthcoming, they asked for and received an extension of six months. Mr. Sumner Welles writes that not only did the Germans fail to deliver the specified items and amounts, but that supervision by the Allied agencies was so lax that Germany was able to arm and equip her ostensible 'police' organizations with more than the usual police weapons, thus forming the nucleus for a future army corps. This must not be allowed to happen in Japan. Disarmament should be easier in Japan, since the smaller size of the country and the concentration of its major industries in a relatively small area will make it possible to supervise closely the whole process without employment of a large or highly skilled United Nations force.

Likewise, the destruction of plants and machinery used for war purposes that cannot be reconverted to peace-time use can be carried out without much difficulty as part of the process of disarmament. Reconversion of war industries to peace-time production, as has been suggested, should be geared to Japanese plans for their postwar economy and need not be hurried. The task of ensuring that reconversion is finally completed by the Japanese should be entrusted to United Nations control agencies established for prevention of rearmament.

The demobilization of Japan's armed forces is not a complex problem. It involves, first of all, their surrender of all arms and equipment and their return to civilian life. It has been proposed that demobilization be regulated with respect to general conditions within Japan and specifically in terms of possibilities of re-employment. Demobilization should not wait, however, upon complete plans by the Japanese for employment of all former soldiers and sailors. It should be carried through in as short a time as possible under supervision of the United Nations occupation authorities, and certainly before occupation forces are withdrawn from the country.

Dissolution of the ex-service men's associations, the militarist organizations, and the patriotic societies should include the formal and public dissolution of these organizations by their officials, and their records should either be confiscated or turned over to United Nations authorities. Most of these organizations and their officers are well known, and enforcement of this ban should not be difficult. Obviously this kind of a penalty is relatively easy to evade, but the value of outlawing these societies, which have been so much a part of Japan's militarism, lies in the fact that a future Japanese government attempting honestly to fulfil the terms of surrender might find it easier to prevent their resurgence if they were banned immediately after surrender.

Similarly, the abolition of the secret police of the Home Office and the gendarmerie of the War Office can be enforced as one of the terms of surrender. Their records can be confiscated or seized by United Nations officials and their reconstitution prohibited. It has been proposed that the United Nations undertake the recruitment and training of such local or provincial police forces as may be necessary for the maintenance of order by a Japanese government after occupation forces have been withdrawn. Abolition of the secret police and the gendarmerie are prerequisite to such an attempt, and a careful examination of their records might reveal much useful information concerning Japanese who could be given authority in police and other matters.

The trial and punishment of Japanese war criminals is a task that should be entrusted to a special agency, as is proposed in the case of Germany. While it may be presumed that those Japanese who are accused of war crimes committed outside of Japan will be brought before national tribunals in the former occupied territories, arrangements will have to be made for their apprehension. Also, special arrangements will have to be made for the trial and punishment of Japanese accused of committing war crimes within Japan. A United Nations War Crimes Commission for Japan will have to be established to supervise the whole process and establish such tribunals as are necessary for conducting these trials.

Additional measures proposed to discredit the militarists, such as the exile and internment of officers, or that all military personnel be held as prisoners of war, are of doubtful value. The psychological effect of such acts on the Japanese people cannot be determined in advance and might be the opposite from that intended. The militarists will partially discredit themselves by losing the war. Their future position and prestige will depend more upon the kind of a Japan that emerges in the future than on any specific actions of the United Nations, other than those directly relating to disarmament, demobilization, and punishment of war criminals outlined above.

The immediate tasks of disarming Japan, destroying her war-making power, and eliminating her armed forces with their supporting civilian organizations can be carried out under the authority of United Nations occupation officials without the necessity of too complex an organization and within a comparatively short time. Experience with similar problems in Germany should be of great assistance, if the war with Japan continues for any period after Germany's final defeat.

It is assumed that the terms of surrender for Japan, or the treaty of peace with a Japanese government, or whatever agreements are made with respect to Japan's postwar status, will include undertakings by Japan to fulfil the conditions of disarmament and the restrictions imposed for prevention of rearmament. The task of enforcement of these provisions over an unspecified 'period of years' is one chiefly of surveillance to determine whether the Japanese are fulfilling the obligations imposed.

Prevention of any Japanese attempt at rearmament will involve a system of inspection within Japan by United Nations authorities for the purpose of detecting violations. Experience with Germany after the last war indicates that it will do little good to search for secret laboratories or drafting rooms or factories where test models of military materials are being constructed. Concealment of such activity is too easy. But no nation can risk war without vast quantities of military equipment and large stockpiles of materials for war purposes. Investigation of any Japanese attempts to rearm should be directed at uncovering any production of armaments in quantity or any stock-piling of material that cannot be shown to be for the production of peace-time goods.

This kind of investigation would demand periodic inspections of Japanese industry and inspection of government records. Importation of any large quantities of raw materials or semi-finished or finished products that might be used for war purposes could be checked both in Japan and by examination of trade statistics of exporting countries. This job would require a relatively small staff of military, industrial, and technical experts with rights of travel and inspection anywhere in Japan, and a group of experts capable of analyzing the information obtained in Japan and from other sources.

Prevention of any aircraft construction, of any aluminum and magnesium production, and of imports of aluminum, alumina, alunite, or bauxite, and limitations on Japan's merchant-ship tonnage would not require additional staff or machinery, since investigation of any violation of these restrictions can be undertaken by the authorities charged with surveillance to prevent rearmament.

The problem of preventing the Japanese from reorganizing their ex-service men's association, their militarist and patriotic societies, and their secret police and gendarmerie is admittedly a more difficult task. It is easy to camouflage the purposes of any organization and conduct much of its activity in secret. It should be possible, however, to keep track of the activities of any very extreme Japanese organizations and any literature they produce, and thus determine whether they are cloaks for military training or militaristic propaganda.

Prevention of rearmament for whatever period is deemed necessary will require the creation of a United Nations Control Commission for Japan, similar to that being proposed for Germany. This Commission will have the task of maintaining a continued surveillance over Japan to insure that the Japanese fulfil the obligations they are forced to accept to prevent their rearmament. If the investigations of the Control Commission reveal evidence that Japan is attempting to rearm or is violating any of the terms of surrender or the restrictions imposed upon her, the Control Commission would have the responsibility of determining what steps should be taken to stop violations and what penalties should be imposed upon Japan for such acts.

To keep the public informed of Japan's progress as a peaceful nation or, contrariwise, of her evasion of postwar obligations, and to provide a focal point for continuing United Nations collaboration, full annual reports of the Control Commission should be required and made public. At two- or three-year intervals, Japan's status should be subject to public review by the Control Commission, to determine whether any restrictions could be modified or removed or whether additional control measures should be adopted. This will provide an opportunity and an incentive for the Japanese to present evidence that they are becoming eligible for full rights in the international community. (Obviously, careful investigation of Japan's evidence will be needed and should be undertaken by the Control Commission.) By thus providing a fixed time and place for Japan to present her case, the United Nations will retain both the initiative and the opportunity for careful consideration of her evidence. Such a procedure will mean a more orderly handling of Japanese pleas for lenience while at the same time lessening the effects of direct Japanese appeals to individual governments and their peoples.

A United Nations Control Commission for Japan, with fixed powers, required to make periodic, public reports of its investigations, coupled with an agreement for review of Japan's status at two- or three-year intervals would tend to check a fatal defect in public attitudes that was observable in the inter-war period. After 1919, too many people viewed the mere establishment of the League of Nations as a guarantee against renewed German aggression. To the public, the League was endowed with a personality, a mind, and a will. It was regarded as a living organism, a super-government, apart from the nations comprising it. Thus, when Germany was known to be violating the disarmament clauses of the Versailles Treaty, the League was blamed for failing to take punitive measures. Such an attitude did not fit the facts, for the League was nothing more or less than an association of nations. Unwillingness of the individual member nations to act, not the failure of the League as an organization, was responsible for the failure to prevent German rearmament.

Any United Nations agencies responsible for preventing Japan's rearmament must be recognized as organs through which the member *nations* are performing a common, agreed task, organs through which the peoples of those member nations have assumed a definite responsibility to be discharged by their governments. Periodic reviews of Japan's status, therefore, can provide one means by which the peoples of the United Nations will be made regularly aware that the maintenance of peace is the continuing responsibility of their governments.

Enforcement of the conditions imposed upon Japan will demand that any violation of the terms of disarmament or the restrictions on rearmament be penalized effectively and promptly. The kinds of penalties to be invoked can either be predetermined at the time of establishment of the Control Commission or agreed upon when any violation actually is proved. The Control Commission should be in the best position to recommend the kinds of penalties most effective in relation to particular violations as they occur.

Obviously it would be unnecessary and perhaps unwise for the United Nations to use armed force against Japan as a penalty for every violation of the restrictions imposed upon her. When a violation occurs, the Control Commission or the United Nations Security Council might issue to the Japanese authorities an order to 'cease and desist.' If it was ascertained that the violations were continuing after issuance of such an order, then penalties of different kinds might be applied in terms of the existing situation. Such penalties might take the form of restrictions on imports and exports, curtailment of credit abroad, limitations on foreign-exchange transactions, or the more drastic action of freezing all trade and assets of the Japanese abroad. If these proved ineffective in stopping Japanese violations, then the use of combined force by the United Nations would be the last resort.

Whatever penalties are used to enforce Japan's compliance with her obligations under the terms of surrender, it is essential that they be the result of common agreement and of common action by the United Nations. Past experience makes it imperative that the penalties be drastic enough to leave no doubt in the minds of the Japanese with regard to United Nations determination to enforce Japan's fulfilment of its obligations. It is equally important that there be no delay in invoking the agreed-upon penalties. Any weakness in enforcing the terms of surrender and the conditions imposed upon Japan to prevent rearmament, or any delay caused by the kind of debates engaged in too often at Geneva would be fatal to prevention of future Japanese aggression. It would give Japan's militarists just the kind of encouragement needed to foster the spirit of revenge among their people and to plan for another war.

Keeping Japan disarmed by enforcement through a United Nations Control Commission of the measures previously discussed is by no means an impossible task. It can be done without too large a staff or too complex an organization. There are no technical obstacles to enforcement that cannot be easily surmounted in most instances. It must be recognized, however, that there are certain political and psychological obstacles to continued control of Japan and these must frankly be faced if Japan is to be 'kept disarmed' and prevented from undertaking future aggression.

It is certain that no matter how lenient or how drastic are the terms of surrender and the restrictions imposed upon Japan after defeat, they will arouse violent protest and much bitterness among the Japanese. It is to be expected that many Japanese will do everything they can to sabotage their enforcement and to evade the fulfilment of these obligations. The Japanese are certain to use every means of propaganda to make the peoples of the United Nations believe that they are being harshly treated and that unless restrictions are modified or removed altogether a developing hatred will cause them to try forcibly to break their bonds.

After the last war, the Germans deliberately fostered the idea that the harsh terms of the Versailles Treaty made it impossible for their government to develop peaceful international relations, and it was alleged that a growing desire for revenge made it possible for Hitler to seize power. Whatever the degree of truth in these assertions, Germany was taken down the road to war by a group of men ambitious to make Germany the dominant nation of the western world. They used any means at hand to achieve their ends and, had the terms of the Versailles Treaty been less harsh, it is certain they would have found other means of mobilizing their people for conquest. This will be equally true of Japan. After this war, any Japanese who desire to re-establish Japan's power and again set their nation on a path of conquest will use any methods at hand to gain these ends. A lenient or a drastic peace will make little difference to their ambitions or actions, but they will attempt to make other people believe that their only desire is to remove the 'unfair' and 'unjust' conditions imposed upon their nation as a result of defeat. If this propaganda line is accepted by people in the United Nations, such acceptance can be an obstacle to continued enforcement, unless it has already been determined that Japanese actions, not words, over a period of time are to be the test of their intentions.

A related obstacle to enforcement will arise if the Japanese are permitted to spread the idea that the restrictions imposed upon them are a barrier to their nation's peaceful development. Before this war, Japan's ruling groups built up the notion among their own people and before the world that the chief causes for their own imperial expansion were foreign restrictions upon their trade and foreign opposition to their 'legitimate' needs. These were made the excuses for conquest abroad and the justifications for failure to deal effectively with urgent problems at home. After this war, Japan, like all other nations, will face complex internal problems, the peaceful solution of which will demand many drastic readjustments in the government and in the economy of the nation. Many Japanese will find it much easier to blame their internal difficulties on the 'harsh' terms of surrender and continued enforcement of these terms by the United Nations than to admit their own unwillingness to risk profits, or power, or prestige, by tackling grave internal problems. They will claim that a solution to Japan's difficulties can be obtained only by a removal of the restrictions or a relaxation of their enforcement. They will not find it hard to make their own people believe this. If they succeed in gaining support for this propaganda abroad, such an attitude could become a grave obstacle to continued enforcement.

These obstacles to enforcement of conditions of surrender are more likely to arise in the event that a seemingly 'peace-minded' and 'liberal' government comes to power in Japan soon after defeat. There will be many people within the United Nations who will demand an immediate relaxation of restrictions before such a government has had an opportunity to prove itself. Likewise, Japanese leaders of such a government may be expected to make the same demand on the grounds that continued enforcement or restrictions against their nation hampers their efforts to achieve a peaceful and democratic development. If they succeeded, it would be an easy way of increasing their prestige at home without the risks involved in putting into practice domestic policies of reform.

Any government in postwar Japan, in fact, that announces itself as 'liberal' and 'democratic' can count upon some sympathy among the peoples within the United Nations, and the continued enforcement of restrictive measures against Japan under such a government will raise objections from her sympathizers abroad. Such wishful thinking in advance of positive proof of the 'liberalism' or 'democracy' of any Japanese government can become a grave obstacle to continued enforcement, which can only be overcome by a careful investigation and public discussion of the facts.

Can Japan be policed indefinitely? In his radio address from

the Puget Sound Navy Yard on August 12, 1944, President
Roosevelt stated:

It is an unfortunate fact that other nations cannot trust Japan.
It is an unfortunate fact that years of proof must pass before we
can trust Japan and before we can classify Japan as a member
of the society of nations which seeks permanent peace and whose
word we can take.

During these 'years of proof' it will be necessary to maintain
and enforce the conditions imposed upon Japan to prevent
her rearmament, but in view of the possible obstacles to continued enforcement discussed above, there would seem to be
some doubt whether the peoples of the United Nations will
support such action indefinitely. It is possible if not probable
that the people within the United Nations will tire of the task
and become more and more receptive to appeals for an end
to a thoroughly unwelcome obligation. When this happens,
the United Nations risk a renewal of Japanese aggression, for
there is little doubt that many Japanese will count on the unwillingness of the United Nations to police their country
over a long period and will foresee in this an opportunity to
revive their military power.

There is only one safeguard against this contingency—the
development of a peaceful and trustworthy Japan. The measures discussed in the preceding chapters will not produce such
a change in Japan, for their objective is a negative one—prevention of renewed aggression. They will provide some assistance, however, in so far as they aid in breaking the political
power of the militarists; but development of a peaceful Japan
depends upon much more than a loss of power by this one
group among Japan's ruling classes. It depends upon drastic
and fundamental political, economic, and social reforms in
which the rigid control of all of Japan's old bosses—militarists,
bureaucrats, politicians, business men, and nobility—must give

way to a new system in which the common people have a
voice.

Political reforms cannot succeed so long as economic
power remains concentrated in the hands of the few, nor can
economic and social reforms succeed so long as the instruments of political power are denied to the many. Japan's future, therefore, must be considered in terms of those reforms
needed to give the Japanese people opportunities to profit by
peace, opportunities so far denied to them, but without which
some Japanese will always seek to profit by war. It is possible
that the Japanese people can achieve this for themselves, but
the odds are heavy against them. These odds can be reduced
if the United Nations adopt positive measures of assistance in
the reform of Japan as the best means, over all others, of in-
suring against future Japanese aggression.

VIII

The Imperial Throne

THE day Japan surrenders, the United Nations must be prepared to decide upon the most fundamental problem of
Japan's future: the postwar status of the Imperial Throne.
This is not merely a question of the position of the present
Emperor, Hirohito, and the Imperial family. It is the larger
problem of an institution which has been the core of the national beliefs, political system, and social structure of seventy
million people.

The policy of the United Nations toward Japan will determine whether the position of the Imperial Throne remains
unchanged, is modified, or is destroyed. This policy must be
decided in advance. It cannot be improvised. How far it has
been determined by responsible officials of the United Nations is uncertain. But it is certain that the problem of the
Emperor has stirred more public interest and discussion
within those United Nations engaged in the struggle against
Japan than any other aspect of Japan's future.

To date there has been little enlightenment on this subject
in official statements. Toward Mussolini and his Fascists and
toward Hitler and his Nazis have been directed some of the
strongest United Nations condemnations, but toward the
Emperor of Japan the United Nations seem strangely neutral.
Derogatory remarks about Hirohito have been forbidden
in United Nations propaganda to Asia. As a result, both the
British Foreign Office and the American State Department
have been charged with preferring to retain the Imperial
Throne as an element of stability in Japan to avoid the revo-

lution which they fear should the Emperor be deposed and the Throne eliminated. Dr. Sun Fo, son of the great Chinese leader Sun Yat-sen and head of China's Legislative Yuan, is the only high United Nations official to have advocated total elimination of the Imperial Throne in favor of a republican form of government for Japan.

Fundamentally, the determination of the future of Japan's Imperial House depends upon the answer to two questions. Is the institution of the Throne, with its myths and traditions, so essential an element of Japanese nationalism as to be inseparable from the political, economic, and social institutions of the nation? Is the continuance of the Imperial Throne compatible with the development of a peaceful Japan in the future? The answers to these questions necessarily must be based upon an understanding of the historical role the Throne has played in Japan's history and upon an estimate of its position in the modern Japanese state.

Early in Japanese history, the primitive inhabitants of the islands developed the legend that they were descendants of divine beings, who had specially selected their islands as the home of a superior race. These legends were closely related to the nature worship of a primitive society composed of clans or tribes, who struggled among themselves for control of fertile spots where they could make a living. In this period, which the Japanese fix as between the fifth and seventh centuries B.C., a strong clan rose to power on the island of Kyushu and later moved to the Yamato district on the main island of Honshu, where it attempted to broaden its power. To accomplish its aim, this clan claimed a special position for its members as direct descendants of the sun-goddess, Amaretasu-Omikami, the diety chiefly responsible in legend for the founding of Japan. Its chief assumed the title and prerogatives of *Tenno*, or 'Heavenly King,' and this 'imperial' clan declared itself to be the sole depository of sovereignty and the source of final authority over the 'Yamato' race.

The authority of the Imperial clan was often challenged, but circumstances of history and political expediency combined to preserve its position and the unbroken continuity of the Imperial House. Other clans, ambitious to expand their control, found it easier to seek Imperial sanction for their actions, or even to force such approval, than to enmesh themselves both in a struggle for power with rival clans and a fight against Imperial traditions that were becoming more strongly embedded in the minds of the people with each generation. The wealth and power of the Imperial clan waxed and waned, but the dynasty and its position as the sole source of authority over the people were never obliterated.

By the end of the sixteenth century, Japan's primitive culture had long since given way to the development of more civilized institutions under the stimulus of contacts with the Chinese and other peoples. Japan had become unified under a succession of powerful clans, which continued to draw their authority from the Imperial Throne. From 1603 until 1867, however, Japan was virtually isolated from the outside world under the rule of the militaristic, autocratic Tokugawa family. For these two and a half centuries, the myths and legends of Japan's divine origin and divinely guided destiny symbolized by the Throne were propagated actively by the Tokugawa as one means of preserving their power. These myths and traditions were documented by records, half-fact, half-fiction, but accepted as authentic history and unchallenged by scientific scholarship. They emphasized the supernatural origin of the Japanese people, their relationship to the Emperor as the 'father' of the Japanese 'family,' and the favored position of the Imperial House as divinely guided descendants of the deities who had founded the nation. Around these myths was constructed a feudal society in which the most prized virtues were the obedience of the vassal to his lord, of the warrior to his commander, the submissiveness of the members of the family to the father, the duties of inferiors to superiors, and the over-all obligation of Japanese subjects to give absolute loyalty to the Emperor.

Japan's national unity came naturally with the development of common customs and a common language among people living in a compact group of islands. But this unity was greatly strengthened by the myths surrounding the Throne, which Japan's leaders, perhaps unconsciously in the beginning, found to be perfect instruments for forging and firmly establishing those beliefs in racial superiority and uniqueness of civilization which we call nationalism. Japanese nationalism, therefore, is deeply rooted in the perpetuation of primitive beliefs, feudal customs, and ritualistic practices built around the existence of a divine emperor, at once the symbol of the country's 'uniqueness' and its 'greatness' as a nation.

This nationalism flourished unscathed by the revolutionary changes in the western world of the eighteenth and nineteenth centuries. Japan's isolation under the Tokugawa immunized the nation from the forceful currents of changing ideas and beliefs that swept through Europe and shook its feudal foundations to produce our modern, western world.

Japan's entry into the modern world after Commodore Perry's visit in 1853 did not change the position of the Throne or greatly modify its myths and traditions. The aristocrats who led Japan into active participation in world affairs in the late nineteenth century sought to retain these ancient beliefs and customs as a means of preserving their control over the people. Absolute loyalty to the Emperor became the primary virtue in a 'modern' Japan, in which the legends and myths of old Japan were actively perpetuated.

From various segments of Japanese society come proof that

the Imperial myths have been made an integral part of the fabric of the national life. In 'modern' Japan, school children are taught that

We subjects who live under such an illustrious Imperial family are for the most part descendants of the gods . . . It is clear that the foundation of our state has been superior from ancient times to that of other countries.

In 'modern' Japan, the Vice-Speaker of the elected House of Representatives can seriously assert,

The Emperor is to the Japanese mind the supreme being in the cosmos of Japan as god is in the universe of the pantheistic philosopher. From Him everything emanates; in Him everything subsists; there is nothing on the soil of Japan existent independent of Him. He is the sole owner of the Empire, the author of law, justice, privilege and honor, and the symbol of the unity of the Japanese nation. He needs no pope or archbishop to crown Him at His accession. He is supreme in all temporal matters and He is the foundation of Japanese social and civil morality.

In 'modern' Japan, Premier Prince Konoye, who has traveled and studied abroad and who has been considered a 'moderate' by some westerners, can safely make the statement that

Our movement must not stop at the creation of a mutual co-prosperity sphere in East Asia alone. We must prosecute the movement for all time and so realize peace and security for the whole world . . . The movement is based on the spirit of the Imperial Way. In short, the basic objective for which the movement is being conducted is for assistance to the Throne.

And in wartime Japan, at public rallies all over the country, a 'people's pledge' is chanted:

We, the subjects of his Imperial Majesty the Emperor shall offer everything we have for the sake of His Imperial Majesty the Emperor; we shall extend the august virtue of His Imperial

Majesty to all corners of the world; we shall certainly win
this war by embracing and protecting the Imperial Throne; we
shall resolutely and absolutely worship His Imperial Majesty the
Emperor; in reverent acceptance of His Imperial Edict we shall
abide by it.

These phrases, which sound strange and even ridiculous to
western ears, do not fail to produce the proper response from
Japanese, whose patriotism and love of country are intricately
bound up with the all-pervading authority of a theocratic
Emperor. The Imperial myths have become part and parcel
of the superstitions, religious beliefs and social customs, which
together form the base for Japan's extreme nationalism.

These basic traditions and myths about the Emperor also
appear in Japan's 'modern' Constitution, promulgated in the
name of the Emperor in 1889, the preamble of which states
in part,

Having, by virtue of the glories of Our Ancestors, ascended
the Throne of a lineal succession unbroken for ages eternal; desiring to promote the welfare of, and give development to the
moral and intellectual faculties of Our beloved subjects, the very
same that have been favored with the benevolent care and affectionate vigilance of Our Ancestors; and hoping to maintain the
prosperity of the State, in concert with Our people and with
their support, We hereby promulgate, in pursuance of Our Imperial Rescript . . . a fundamental law of State, to exhibit the
principles by which We are to be guided in Our conduct, and
to point out what Our descendants and Our subjects and their
descendants are forever to conform.

The rights of sovereignty of the State, We have inherited from
Our Ancestors, and We shall bequeath them to Our descendants . . .

The first sixteen articles of the Constitution deal with the
Emperor, his position, powers, and prerogatives. Three of
them are particularly important:

Article I: The Empire of Japan shall be reigned over and governed by a line of Emperors unbroken for ages eternal.

Article III: The Emperor is sacred and inviolable.

Article IV: The Emperor is the head of the Empire, combining in himself the rights of sovereignty, and exercises them, according to the provisions of the present constitution.

This 'modern' Constitution preserves in its text all of the old ideas of Emperor-divinity, the position of the Throne as the sole source of authority, and the obligation of all subjects to conform to the Imperial will. It is the gift of the Emperor to his subjects, not the product of the people's will. No amendments can be made save on the initiative of the Emperor. The important powers to make war, conclude peace, approve treaties, and legislate in emergencies are reserved to the Emperor. All laws passed by the national legislature, the Imperial Diet, must receive Imperial approval before they become effective, and should this approval be withheld there is no provision for overriding the Imperial veto. Under the Constitution, the vital powers of government have been vested in the Emperor, not in the representatives of the people in the Diet.

But the real position of the Emperor is quite different than his legal, constitutional position. Although possessing large powers and extensive authority under the Constitution, Japan's modern emperors have never been permitted to exercise their constitutional powers. Instead, the Imperial Throne has been the symbol of unity and the Emperor has been the source of authority used by the real rulers of Japan—the militarists, bureaucrats, politicians, nobility, and industrial monopolists—to imprison the Japanese people in a rigidly controlled society to serve the purposes of militarism and imperialism. There is no evidence that any emperor under the Constitution has exercised more than an evanescent influence over affairs of state. Rather, the real bosses of Japan bend the

Emperor to their will, for he is part and parcel of the autocratic, controlled society they have created, and the Throne
is the hub around which their totalitarian system revolves.

The significance of the Throne as an inseparable part of
Japanese nationalism has been well summarized in the following statement:

Thus, whether we choose to regard the modern Japanese emperors as puppets, partial puppets or even active political partic-
ipants in the affairs of state, the institution has shown itself unable
to check the course of Japanese political and military aggression.
On the contrary, the Emperor institution in the hands of several
generations of Japanese statesmen and bureaucrats, variously described as liberal, moderate or reactionary, has been the chosen
instrument to indoctrinate the people with a racism as malignant
as Nazism, with an unscientific tribal exclusiveness, and with a
contempt for human life whether Japanese or foreign that has
nothing in common with the qualities of courage or sacrifice since
it is nourished by an in-human and anti-social fanaticism. This
institution has invariably served as the magic charm, which in
the hands of those who have guided Japanese policy for the past
fifty years, has dazzled, beguiled and finally debauched the minds
of all but the most heroically humane and intelligent Japanese.[1]

In the western world, beliefs in divine rule and supernatural
authority have been generally discarded as a basis for modern
government, and the king in a constitutional monarchy remains only as a symbol of the nation's unity. In Japan, the
Emperor is both a symbol of unity and an institution inseparable from the political, economic, and social structure of the
nation, an institution historically the keystone of Japan's militaristic and aggressive nationalism.

Proceeding from the conclusion that the Imperial Throne
plays a vital part in the political, economic, and social institutions of the Japanese nation, it remains to be determined

[1] 'A Canadian View,' *Pacific Affairs*, June 1944.

whether retention of the Emperor will be compatible with
the development of a peaceful Japan. While it can be confi-
dently asserted, for instance, that retention of large armed
forces by Japan after the war would not be conducive to her
peaceful development, it cannot be stated with equal cer-
tainty that retention of the Throne in postwar Japan will be
a barrier to such development. The extent and variety of
views on this problem can best be indicated in a summary of
the arguments that have been presented in favor of and against
retention of the Emperor. Those advocating the retention of
the Throne are as follows:

1. It is asserted that the use of the Imperial myths and traditions by Japanese nationalists to gain support for extreme
militarism is a comparatively recent phenomenon. With the
defeat of Japan, the elimination of the army and navy, and
a resulting loss of militarist prestige, it is contended that these
myths and traditions will become less important, and eventually will cease to be the chief basis for national actions. It is
held that they have been dangerous to peace only in the hands
of the militarists and hence will not be a hindrance to the
growth of peaceful, non-aggressive policies in a postwar
Japan shorn of militarist domination.

2. It is asserted that the Imperial Throne is the single stabilizing element in Japanese society and that to attack this institution or to attempt to eliminate it would risk throwing
the whole country into chaos or violent revolution. It is contended that any postwar Japanese government will need the
support of Imperial authority to maintain itself in power and
to obtain compliance with its policies and its orders to assure
necessary reforms and reconstruction.

3. It is contended that the Throne should not be done
away with because, in modern Japan, the Imperial system is
'in itself passive, a true tool.' It is admitted that the Emperor
and the Imperial myths have been used as a tool by the mili-

tarists and their nationalists supporters in the past, but it is asserted that the Throne can be used equally well by the more moderate and liberal Japanese leaders for the development of peaceful policies.

4. It is also asserted that the United Nations may be able to 'use' the Imperial Throne, not only to sanction the terms of surrender and Japan's disarmament and demilitarization, but also to initiate those minimum political, economic, and social reforms needed to start the Japanese down the road to a peaceful future. It has been suggested, for example, that the United Nations might depose Hirohito, establish a Regency in favor of his young son, and, by selecting the Regent, use the Imperial authority for their purposes.

The foregoing arguments hold that the Imperial institution is not dangerous to a peaceful Japan, but that on the contrary, the Imperial Throne can be useful to the Japanese and to the United Nations in the reconstruction of the country and its development of peaceful policies. To each of these arguments, however, strong objections have been raised within the United Nations. The counter-arguments can be summarized as follows:

1. It is asserted that the Imperial myths and traditions are an inseparable part of Japanese institutions, which not only the militarists, but all elements of the ruling classes have used to perpetuate a feudal, militaristic society. It is contended that nothing short of fundamental reform of this whole society will make possible the growth of a peaceful Japan and that, therefore, retention of the Throne and its myths will constitute a major barrier to reform and a constant focal point for those Japanese who will desire in the future to revive their national meglomania.

2. It is admitted that the Throne has provided a basis for Japanese unity and in this sense has been a stabilizing element within the nation. But it is asserted that historically, in both

ancient and modern times, the Throne has been the base for a rigidly controlled, static society, upon which has been reared one of the most ruthless militarisms of modern times. It is contended that transformation of such an institution into a base for liberal, democratic, and peaceful development is an impossibility, even under the most favorable conditions.

3. It is contended that the Emperor is not a passive tool, a neutral agency that can be operated by any group for whatever purposes it desires. On the contrary, it is asserted that the Emperor has been the tool only of coalitions of the ruling classes that were able at the moment to command political control of the government. As the tool exclusively of the ruling classes, it is held that the Throne has been fashioned to fit the hands of Japan's autocrats and empire builders, that the Throne has always been a mechanism of reaction, not reform. It is asserted that historically, liberal elements in Japan have never been able to use the Emperor, but on the contrary have always sought to deflate the Imperial myths, circumscribe the authority of the Emperor, and make of the Cabinet and the elected House of Representatives the organs of popular will and the responsible political agencies through which, alone, internal reforms and peaceful foreign policies could be obtained.

4. It is contended that for the United Nations to support and acknowledge the authority of the Throne as an alternative to disorder or revolution would be to place a sanction of inestimable value on a system by which Japan's real rulers have led their nation on a course of aggression and would plan to do so again. Such a policy, it is affirmed, would enable these leaders to absolve the Emperor for Japan's defeat and to preserve the Imperial institution for use at some future time when oportunity for new conquest presents itself.

The most noteworthy statement in opposition to retention of the Throne has been made by Dr. Sun Fo, President of

China's Legislative Yuan in an article, 'The Mikado Must Go' (*Foreign Affairs*, October 1944). Dr. Sun summarizes the argument as follows:

If Hirohito must be absolved in the eyes of the Japanese people from the guilt for a disastrous war by admitting that he was powerless to correct the errors of his subordinates, what will be the value of the Imperial Rescript for the introduction of democracy by the Will of Heaven? On the other hand, if from our point of view the Emperor is in fact blameless but nevertheless so powerful a force that he must be kept and 'used,' why was he not able to rally the better elements among his people during the past decade and to check the militarists who were imposing policies of which he disapproved? . . . The 'hands-off-the-Mikado' school cannot have it both ways. The Mikado is either a puppet and is useless for purposes of democracy; or he is powerful and should have disciplined his militarists. He cannot be both. Either way he is a malevolent factor . . . Democracy by Imperial Rescript would be nothing less than a continuation of the Japanese game of hoodwinking the world . . . There is no short-cut to democracy. Democracy lies in the will of the people to rule themselves. Its source cannot be the will of a Mikado, whether or not he is thought to be a god.

In addition to these various views for and against retention of the Emperor the opinion has been expressed in several quarters that the United Nations should 'wait and see' how the Japanese react to defeat before formulating a policy toward the Throne. The most distinguished proponent of this view is Under-Secretary of State Joseph C. Grew, former American Ambassador to Japan. In testimony before the Senate Foreign Relations Committee on December 12, 1944, Mr. Grew voiced his belief that any decision on this question should be delayed until United Nations forces have occupied Japan.

While from many standpoints it would appear easier to

postpone a decision on this most difficult and controversial question, the experience of the United Nations in Europe would seem to indicate the danger of such delay. Not only are there formidable difficulties to be faced in trying to improvise policies on the spot, but the possibilities of serious public misunderstanding and objections both within Japan and in the United Nations should not be overlooked.

Among the difficulties that a 'wait and see' policy may create is the assumption by the Japanese that official silence by the United Nations implies their approval of the Imperial system, with resulting initial discouragement to any Japanese groups who may desire to work for the Throne's elimination. Furthermore, relationships once established between occupying authorities and the Imperial Throne will tend to become commitments from which it will be increasingly difficult to withdraw, and unwittingly the United Nations may become allied against liberal groups, who will suspect and distrust the motives of the United Nations and hence may refuse or make difficult the co-operation necessary to peaceful reforms.

The inescapable conclusion is that the United Nations must now decide that the Throne and its myths cannot safely be adapted to the needs of a peaceful Japan and must be relegated to history along with the archaic society, autocratic government, and totalitarian economy it has supported. The issue resolves itself into the problem of how best to eliminate this institution and the part that the United Nations should play in the process. There are two alternatives. Either the United Nations can abolish the Throne at the time of occupation, or they can adopt a policy of assistance to those Japanese willing to work for its eventual elimination.

There is much to be said in favor of summary abolition of the Throne, either as one of the terms of surrender, or as an act of the occupying authorities immediately after defeat. Its immediate abolition would eliminate the danger that Japan's former militarists would use it to gain popular support for renewed militarism and aggression. It could force the Japanese to set about the reconstruction of their political system upon a wholly new basis and within a framework of political principles that the United Nations consider necessary to her development as a trustworthy nation. Immediate abolition of the Throne would also provide the opportunity for many Japanese to develop a stake in a different kind of government, which they would be willing to defend against restoration of the old order and which they would be unwilling to subject to the risks of empire-building.

On the other hand, it is quite possible that abolition of the Throne by the United Nations would serve to make the Imperial family martyrs in the eyes of the Japanese people and would so intensify their hatred against their former enemies, particularly against the United States, as to make construction of a new governmental system impossible. The Japanese people might regard the abolition of the Throne as such an unwarranted and unnecessary attack upon their most sacred national institution that they would refuse to co-operate with any liberal groups who wished to take advantage of United Nations assistance in the trying tasks of political, economic, and social reform. If this occurred, the United Nations would face the problem of either continuing to occupy and administer Japan indefinitely or of modifying the original policy. Or, if a new government was formed, many Japanese might regard such a regime as a puppet of the United Nations, and their compatriots in such a government as 'collaborators' with their former enemies. The United Nations would then be in the position of supporting a government that lacked inherent stability and would collapse as soon as their support was withdrawn.

In any event, and no matter what the reactions of the Japanese people to United Nations abolition of the Throne, the

United Nations would have to be prepared to assume continuing and indefinite responsibilities beyond those necessary to initial disarmament and demilitarization. These responsibilities would involve not only active support of Japanese groups willing to take over the reins of a new government, but also active participation in the construction of such a government, in the maintenance of law and order, and in reorganizing the nation's economic and social institutions to the extent necessary to set up the new system. No one can predict how long the United Nations would have to occupy and administer Japan in order to give the new regime a chance to establish itself and to survive after United Nations occupations forces were withdrawn.

The disadvantages of direct United Nations abolition of the Imperial Throne would seem to outweigh the advantages. For if it is true, as Dr. Sun Fo states, that democracy cannot be instituted by Imperial Rescript, then it is equally true that democracy and peaceful development cannot be instituted successfully by United Nations fiat. Therefore, the only other alternative is a comprehensive policy of positive United Nations assistance to those Japanese who are prepared to reform their institutions and re-order their national beliefs so as to make possible and desirable the elimination of the Throne by their own efforts.

The first step in a policy of assisting the Japanese to get rid of the Emperor and the Imperial ideology is for the United Nations to make every effort to obtain the Emperor's approval of the terms of surrender, of any peace treaty or subsequent agreements necessary to Japan's total defeat, total disarmament, and total demilitarization. The Emperor should be 'used' as fully as possible to document Japan's crushing defeat, and the Throne should be held as fully responsible for Japanese aggression as the militarists. Full publicity within Japan should be given to the Emperor's acknowledgment of responsibility for the loss of the war, so as to leave no doubt in the minds of the Japanese people that the United Nations regard the Imperial institution as a vital part of Japan's militaristic system which must be done away with.

The second step is for United Nations authorities to avoid any acts during occupation which might of themselves indicate that it was United Nations policy to retain and support the Throne in postwar Japan or which might be an acknowledgment in the eyes of the Japanese of the Emperor's sanctity and traditional position. United Nations authorities should refuse to be received in audience by the Emperor or to attend any ceremonies in his presence or any connected with glorification of the Imperial traditions. They should oppose any Japanese groups that use the old shibboleths of Emperor-divinity or of blind obedience to 'the injunctions of the divine ancestors.'

A third and more positive step would be for the United Nations occupation authorities to 'by-pass' the Emperor completely in the administration of Japanese areas under occupation. Authority could be given directly to local Japanese officials, laws could be enforced and taxes collected without reference to Imperial ordinances, statutes, or approval. The source and ultimate enforcing power would come from the United Nations Control Commission for Japan. Such a policy would demonstrate to the Japanese people that government could function and laws could be promulgated and enforced without reference to the Emperor, and this demonstration might make it easier for the Japanese to re-constitute their government upon a sound democratic basis.

To make this policy more effective, the United Nations should consider the advisability of two additional proposals, either or both of which would further aid the Japanese in reforming their political system. First, it has been suggested that the United Nations remove the whole Imperial family from Japan and intern them for an indefinite period in some safe and comfortable country estate, so that the Japanese people would be forced to do without their Emperor during the immediate postwar period when opportunity for fundamental reforms in their political structure will be given them. If, at a future date, the United Nations were satisfied with Japan's government and the Japanese had shown peaceful intentions by their actions, the Imperial family could be safely returned to Japan as an ex-ruling family, if the Japanese people so desired.

Second, it has been suggested that the United Nations assist the Japanese to prepare for a constitutional convention, whose members would be chosen in a democratic election for the purpose of drafting a new organic law for the country. Any revision of the existing Constitution would have to receive Imperial approval, because the Emperor alone has the constitutional right to initiate amendments and because the document itself is his gift to his subjects. For this reason alone an entirely new constitution should be drafted. This could be brought about by making a constitutional convention for this purpose a condition of the peace treaty with Japan, or a prerequisite to the reopening of normal relations between Japan and individual members of the United Nations. (See Chapter IX for specific proposals on constitutional reform.)

It may be that the whole question of the Emperor will not prove important in postwar Japan as seems likely from our knowledge of the position of the Imperial Throne in Japanese life. It should be pointed out that for a period in the late 'twenties there was a half-hearted attempt to popularize Emperor Hirohito before the people and to remove some of the aura of divinity surrounding him. Although this attempt was not very successful, it has been asserted by persons of long residence in Japan that many Japanese do not possess strong convictions or beliefs with regard to the Emperor or the Imperial traditions. Consequently it is argued that the Japanese people can be persuaded to forget what they have been taught without too much difficulty.

More important, perhaps, was the support gained for the political theories of Professor Minobe after the First World War. He maintained that the Emperor was not the sole depository of sovereign power but was only an agent of the people in whom ultimate sovereignty in the Japanese state resided. It is possible that the eventual elimination of the Imperial Throne may not be too difficult for the Japanese to undertake themselves, but it cannot be too strongly emphasized that so long as the Imperial Throne remains in Japan it will be a constant source of danger of a revival of extreme nationalism and a rallying point for the perpetuation of militarism. All the ex-militarists and super-patriots who may be pushed aside in postwar Japan will huddle around the Throne and its traditions as a base for a new bid for power. Elimination of the Emperor-institution in Japan will take away the keystone of the militarist-imperialist system, an essential prelude to peaceful development.

Whatever attitude Japanese groups may take on the position of the Emperor after defeat, the best guarantee of the final elimination of the Imperial Throne as a source of autocratic authority, extreme nationalism, and aggressive militarism will be the inauguration of those fundamental political, economic, and social reforms designed to give the Japanese people opportunity for self-expression and a means of control over their government's policies. It is essential that United Nations authorities be prepared to assist any Japanese liberal groups in initiating these reforms during the period of occupation. Espousal of the concept of complete popular sovereignty as against the old Imperial authority can be the major test of the sincerity of any Japanese groups seeking recognition and assistance from the United Nations in a program of reform.

The policies and actions proposed for the United Nations in the foregoing discussion will not be easy to follow, for they will require accurate and continuing evaluation of conditions within Japan after defeat and of the influence and intentions of various Japanese groups seeking political control. Courage will be required of United Nations officials to act in the face of opposition both from the Japanese and from groups within the different United Nations who will prejudge both policy and actions without giving them a fair trial. Obviously there is no guarantee that any policy will be successful in starting the Japanese on the road to becoming a peaceful and trustworthy nation. However, those who advocate support of the Imperial Throne as a stabilizing factor in Japan after defeat, and those who espouse a 'hands-off' or 'wait and see' policy toward the Emperor, unwittingly or knowingly range themselves on the side of reaction and extreme nationalism. Either they are afraid of chaos or revolution in Japan, or they fear that their own leadership cannot command the necessary home support for United Nations assumption of responsibility for the fundamental transformation of the Japanese nation.

For the United Nations to support the Imperial Throne in Japan after the war, either actively or by their official silence on the subject, is to strengthen an institution subversive of all the principles and aims for which this war is being fought. The ultimate goal of a transformed Japan, willing to live at peace with her neighbors, must not be compromised by attempts to gain the short-term advantage of a temporary stability, which will prevent the Japanese people from freeing themselves at the earliest possible moment from the shackles of an extreme nationalism of which the Imperial Throne is the key.

IX

Political Reconstruction

IF the present ruling classes in Japan are permitted to retain
their control over the nation after defeat, they will inevitably
work for the maintenance of Japan's autocratic political and
economic institutions. They will inevitably work to maintain
their political and economic position by a revival of their nation's armed strength. Japan's rulers have no interest in the
development of popular government or an economy directed
toward advancing the welfare of the whole population, for
such changes would be destructive of their power and restrictive of their economic profits. The hope for a peaceful Japan
lies, first of all, in a thoroughgoing reconstruction of the nation's political system and the development of a popular government in which the nation's leaders can be held responsible
to the people rather than to the Imperial Throne.

Because for two decades the Japanese wilfully misled the
western world into believing that their 'modern' political system was capable of democratic growth and that only the
militarists among the ruling classes were responsible for aggression, it is necessary to examine the nature of this 'modern'
government and the manner in which the ruling classes have
operated it to serve their selfish ends.

Japan's modern rulers, the men who run the government,
operate the economy, and boss the people, compose a relatively small and exclusive circle, engaged in playing for the
stakes of political power within a governmental system of
their own designing. They come from five groups within
Japanese society—the militarists, the industrial monopolists,

the bureaucrats, professional politicians, and the nobility. These groups are the ruling classes in Japan. Labor leaders, intellectuals, peasants or farmers, and other men of the people are not admitted to this select company unless they espouse the traditions of autocracy and feudalism that these modern ruling classes have inherited and purposely preserve.

Some of Japan's rulers or 'bosses' are the managers of the big family business monopolies. A typical representative of big business is Ginjiro Fujihara, one of the managers of the giant Mitsui combine. He held the key post of Minister of Munitions in the War Cabinet of General Koiso. A few business men have reached the top from common beginnings, like Yoshisuke Aikawa, who with the help of the army worked up in the business world to head the large Manchurian Heavy Industries Corporation. Some of the bosses have been professional politicians, like Yuko (Lion) Hamaguchi, who as Premier refused to compromise with the ardent militarists and was consequently assassinated in 1930. Some have been professional bureaucrats, like Koki Hirota, who has held the premiership and the post of Foreign Minister. Less able but much more amenable than Hamaguchi, Hirota has so far escaped assassination. Some bosses have come from the nobility, like Prince Fumimaro Konoye, who has been three times Premier of Japan since 1931 and is still an important figure in politics.

Many of Japan's bosses are militarists. They may be, like General Sadao Araki or Admiral Nobumasa Suetsugu, patriotic firebrands who scorned parties and parliament and urged conquest by war on every occasion. Or, there are more conservative militarists, like Admiral Baron Kataro Suzuki, former President of the Privy Council, who became Japan's third war Premier in April 1945. He is known as one of the 'moderates' among the ruling oligarchy. The first two war Premiers, General Hideki Tojo and his successor, General

Kuniaki Koiso, are examples of the clever, ruthless, but intelligent militarist, trained in the political proving grounds of Korea and Manchuria.

Whatever the background, characteristics, or capacities of Japan's rulers, they have consistently had two points of common interest. First, they have never differed significantly over the goals of Japanese policy, namely, the expansion of Japanese power and domination throughout Asia. But they have differed often on the means to these ends. Some have urged action and some have advocated caution. Some have been timid and some have been bold. Some have wanted to follow the slow process of expansion by economic and political methods and others have wanted rapid conquest by force. All have agreed that their nation must become the dominant, controlling power throughout the Far East.

Second, Japan's bosses have a common interest in the maintenance of their system of autocratic rule over the people, involving the preservation of the rigidly controlled society by means of which they derive their profits and power. The acceptance of this system is the primary requisite of admission to their select company. They are bound together in a kind of collective dictatorship—a boss rule—revolving around the Throne, the source of their authority and the sanction of their aims. Japan's rulers have never permitted their differences of opinion to go to the extreme of endangering the system by which they dictate the political, economic, and social life of the nation.

The group that rules Japan at any one time is a coalition of bosses—composed of militarists, big business men, bureaucrats, politicians, or nobility—who can agree upon a common policy, who have been able by persuasion, bribery, or bullying to gain the support of their most influential colleagues and temporarily to stifle any opposition. This collective dictatorship is constantly changing, since it rests upon a system

of complex compromises among representatives of special interests. In this peculiar system, endless discussion among the
bosses in power and all aspiring bosses is necessary to produce that final compromise that commands real support and
gives real power to the ruling group of the moment. Responsibility for the exercise of power can never be definitely fixed
in such a system, since it is always divided among a number
of men. Japan's bosses rule by dictatorship but no one among
them has yet become a dictator.

Whatever group controls the government, however, pos-
sesses unquestioned power to dictate the lives of Japan's people. For they represent the big family monopolies which hold
the wealth of the nation. They represent the extensive military organizations which can police the nation. They represent the corps of trained men who can operate the complex
governmental agencies. Above all they have been given Imperial approval for their policies, their orders are the commands of the Emperor to his faithful, obedient, and loyal subjects who have never known any other life than that of
vassalage to their Emperor's will.

The power of Japan's rulers does not need to rest upon
control of any organs of popular government. Japan's bosses
do not maintain their power by control of a political party,
although such control, when possible, is useful as a means of
smoothing the way for their policies in the Diet. Their power
does not depend upon political platforms or upon political
organizations that can get out the vote on election day, for
the people have no effective means of calling them to account. Rather, Japan's bosses maintain their power through
their personal prestige and influence with their colleagues
among the ruling classes.

Japan's bosses wield their political power mainly through
the non-legislative agencies of the government, which the
Japanese people have no means of holding responsive to their

will. Most important of these agencies is the Cabinet, composed of the Ministers who head the various government departments and those appointed without portfolio because of their prestige or influence. It is in the Cabinet that primary decisions on domestic and foreign policy are finally made and reported to the Emperor for his approval. But unlike the Cabinet in a parliamentary system of government such as Britain's, the Japanese Cabinet is directly responsible to the Emperor as well as to the Diet. This constitutes an important limitation on legislative control of government policy, a control made even more difficult by the special status enjoyed by the War and Navy Ministers. Under an Imperial Ordinance of 1909, these two posts must be held by a general and an admiral on the active service list recommended by the top-ranking army and navy officers. Because under the Constitution the Emperor is commander-in-chief of the army and navy, the War and Navy Ministers as members of the armed services hold themselves directly responsible to him rather than to the Diet, as do other members of the Cabinet. This has given Japan's militarists a special bargaining position in obtaining approval of their policies and legislative measures. If the Diet refuses to approve a Cabinet measure that would normally call for formation of a new Cabinet able to command majority support in the Diet, the War and Navy Ministers can refuse to resign until the Diet has accepted the militarists' demands or an acceptable compromise has been reached. Or in the formation of a new Cabinet, the army and navy can refuse to designate the War and Navy Ministers until their demands are met, or again, the army and navy may threaten to have their ministers resign and thus lead to the downfall of the whole Cabinet.

The ruling oligarchy also exercises its power through the important *Privy Council*, which under the Constitution is the advisory organ to the Emperor on matters pertaining to Imperial succession or the establishment of a regency, on all Imperial ordinances and legislative measures, and on any matter of policy which the Emperor or Prime Minister specify. The Privy Council is also the final authority for interpretation of the Constitution. Membership in the Privy Council is for life, and while in office Cabinet members are ex-officio members. Privy Councillors are nominated by the Premier, but their appointments, made by the Emperor, must be approved by the Council itself. In the past, most Councillors have been members of the nobility, ex-Cabinet Ministers or high-ranking officers of the army and navy.

Formerly, the *Genro* or Elder Statesmen were the most influential group of advisers to the Emperor. This was an extra-legal body composed of the aristocrats who led in the establishment of Japan's modern government after the Meiji restoration. The death of the last of the Genro, Prince Saionji, in 1940, ended this formerly important institution. Its apparent heir is the group of Cabinet Advisers who are chiefly ex-premiers and other representatives of the ruling classes.

Because of their special relations to the Emperor, the Minister of the Imperial Household and the Lord Keeper of the Privy Seal have been particularly effective channels of influence. Beyond the former's responsibility for affairs of the Imperial family and the latter's for affixing the Imperial and State seals to Imperial ordinances and to acts of the Diet, these officials arrange all audiences with the Emperor and can prevent the views of political opponents of the ruling coalition from reaching his ears.

With respect to war policies, Japan's ruling coalition has operated through the Supreme War Council, on which sit leading army and navy officers and Cabinet Ministers, and through the Imperial Headquarters, a temporary wartime policy agency, also composed of high Cabinet and military officials. The Imperial Headquarters has a special importance because it is presided over by the Emperor in person, and many experts believe it to be the most vital wartime policy-making organ. Neither of these war advisory groups is responsible to the Diet. Like the Cabinet, the Privy Council, and other advisory groups, they are the agencies through which the bosses seek the approval of the Imperial Throne for their various policies.

While boss rule in Japan operates by a system of continuous compromise among the members of the Cabinet and other non-legislative bodies responsible to the Emperor, the bosses must still go to the national legislature for initial approval of appropriations and other legislation by which they can make their policies effective. Normally, it is the legislature that provides a check on boss rule and a means by which the people can call their leaders to account. The aristocrats who framed Japan's Constitution, however, carefully restricted the legislative power in Japan.

Under the Constitution, general legislative power is vested in the Imperial Diet, consisting of the House of Peers and the House of Representatives. The House of Peers, with approximately 400 members, includes men from the Imperial family, the nobility, appointees of the Emperor who have distinguished themselves in service to the state, and a group elected from the highest taxpayers in each prefecture, the principal local administrative division. The House of Representatives consists of 466 members elected by approximately 14,000,000 voters under a system of universal manhood suffrage established in 1925. The national legislature has been a forum for the expression of many views and opinions, but free debate is stifled by traditional controls that make too sharp criticism of government policy an act of disloyalty to the Emperor, and by an oppressive atmosphere in which 'thought control' and the operations of secret police and super-patriotic groups often make free expression a source of physical danger.

Specific constitutional restrictions have prevented the Diet from becoming an organ of popular government and have kept it under control of the ruling coalition. All matters pertaining to the Imperial family, such as succession to the Throne and the institution of a regency, are regulated by the Imperial House Laws, separate from the Constitution and not subject to Diet action. Amendments to the Constitution must receive approval of both Houses of the Diet, but they can only be initiated by the Emperor. All legislation must receive the Emperor's approval, attested by the Imperial seal on the proper documents. In practice, this has made possible the exercise of an absolute veto power over legislation. For Japan's bosses can advise the Emperor to withhold approval of any legislation they object to, or the Cabinet can simply fail to have the law printed in the *Official Gazette*, the final step required to make it effective. Or again, the Cabinet can refuse to request appropriations for carrying out the Diet's legislation, and thus nullify its effect.

More significantly the Diet's power is rigidly curtailed in the matter of appropriations. Neither House can initiate appropriation bills, which must be drawn up and presented by the Cabinet. There is no Diet control over such fixed expenditures as salaries of officials and ordinary expenses of the civilian branches of the administration, the army, or the navy. If the Diet should refuse to pass the Cabinet's budget or any appropriation measure, the Constitution provides that the previous year's budget shall continue in effect automatically. Thus, members of the Diet frequently debate the Cabinet's budget at great length, but few Diets have refused to pass the bills in the end, since such action has little effect on the Cabinet, which, if it desires, can advise the Emperor to dissolve the House of Representatives and order a general election. Japan's Diet, therefore, lacks the most essential power of popular government, the 'power of the purse.'

The constitutional make-up of the Diet is another deterrent to its development into a popular legislative body. Since the House of Peers is composed exclusively of representatives of the ruling classes, Japan's bosses always possess means of controlling one house of the legislature, and under the Constitution the House of Peers has equal legislative power with the elected House of Representatives. Any attempt of the people's representatives to reflect the will of their constituents, if it should run contrary to that of Japan's ruling groups, can be easily blocked in the Upper House of the Diet.

Political parties have existed in Japan since before the Constitution was promulgated, but for the most part they have been tools used by rival groups of aspiring bosses to control the Diet, influence the Cabinet, and thus enhance their power. Because it has been a common misconception in the West that the existence of a political party system in Japan was a portent of growing democracy, a brief survey of the role of political parties is necessary.

Between the first session of the Diet in 1890 and 1918, the government was headed by eight men who passed the premiership around among themselves as if it were a hereditary office. All of these men were aristocrats and for the first thirty years of Japan's modern political history they and their colleagues among the aristocracy dominated the government, controlled the growing army and navy, and led the various political parties that rose and fell during the period. In these thirty years the pattern of party politics was set. It was the politics of leaders, not principles, and systematic organization was lacking. Charges of corruption were frequently made against both leaders and party members. The leaders changed their allegiance often, joining old parties or forming new ones and usually taking their immediate followers with them without much regard for party platforms or principles. Little attempt was made to elicit a large party membership or to develop party loyalty among the electorate.

Between 1918 and 1931, Japan had a series of party governments in which the premiers were active party leaders and in most cases commanded a majority in the House of Representatives. Two fairly stable party organizations, the *Seiyukai* and the *Minseito*, alternately controlled the House for most of this period. Foreign observers were quick to see in this development the growth of a more democratic government. But in reality, a fundamental shift in the ruling classes was occurring, not a transition to popular government. By 1918 the aristocratic bosses of the previous period had died or were too old or tired for active politics, and new bosses were taking their places. These new bosses came from the army and the navy, represented the big business monopolies, or were bureaucrats or professional politicians, and they had no intention of relinquishing their prerogatives in favor of more representative government.

Japan's bosses in the 'twenties manipulated the party organizations to suit their will. The *Seiyukai* became identified with the powerful Mitsui interests and the *Minseito* with the rival Mitsubishi interests, serving the ends of these big businesses rather than the will of the electorate. The prestige of the militarists had fallen as a result of their unsuccessful attempt to dominate Siberia and Manchuria in 1918 and because of charges of maladministration of army funds. The civilian bosses, therefore, had a freer hand than previously, but they used the same old methods to exercise their power.

All of the premiers of this period, of whom only one was an aristocrat, maintained their Cabinets in office, not by relying solely on majority support from the people's elected representatives in the House, but by making political deals, as their predecessors had before them, with groups in the House of Peers, with influential members of the Privy Council, with army and navy leaders, and with members of rival political parties. Of the nine premiers holding office before 1932, only three can be called outstanding party leaders and statesmen—Kei Hara, Yuko Hamiguchi, and Ki Inukai. All three were assassinated while in office by representatives of the extreme nationalists, who disliked their refusal to bow to the will of the militarists and their attempts to act as responsible office-holders with the broader interests of the nation in view.

Obviously the pattern of party politics during these years was little changed from the previous period. Political leaders and party politicians proved themselves incapable and unwilling to make of the political parties instruments of efficient government and organs of popular will. Since this period was one in which there was a good deal of ferment over modern ideas introduced from the West, attempts were made through the Diet to enact social and labor legislation as a primary step toward alleviating the conditions of the Japanese people as a whole. The political leaders of the 'twenties generally resisted these attempts and when forced to approve some measures of social legislation generally contrived through their bureaucratic henchmen to prevent their effective enforcement. Charges of graft and corruption against the political parties involving Cabinet members were aired in the press but were quietly hushed up by the bosses. If the Japanese people had entertained any hope that political parties could be used to end boss rule, the experience of the 'twenties was sadly disillusioning to them and undoubtedly was a reason for more widespread interest in and support of Fascist and Nazi ideas in the decade that followed.

After Japan's armies invaded Manchuria in September 1931, the militarists began using every means at their disposal to increase their power in the government in order to mobilize the nation for greater conquests. The spread of violent nationalism, the use of terrorism against all opponents of forceful expansion, and frequent assassinations marked the political history of the next ten years. Political parties became more and more the tools of the militarists and their henchmen, who were gradually rising to dominance in the government. Finally, the militarists, with the active support of their civilian colleagues among the ruling classes, decided that the old party system was a hindrance to their plans for war mobilization. After the outbreak of hostilities in China in 1937, the bosses began to revamp the political system in preparation for the 'crisis' years ahead. When Prince Konoye, one of the few representatives of the nobility among Japan's recent bosses, took office on July 22, 1940, his Cabinet undertook a thorough 'renovation' of the nation's 'political structure,' aided by the military hierarchy who sought to stamp out once and for all any vestiges of democratic government left in the old party system.

The Konoye Cabinet announced the abolition of all political parties as 'incompatible with our national polity' because they were founded on principles of 'liberty, democracy, or socialism.' In his speech inaugurating the 'new' political structure, he announced:

The aim of the new national structure is to unite all the forces of the State and people, welding into one living whole our hundred million fellow countrymen and enabling them to fulfill in the highest degree their duty as subjects of the Throne . . . For the successful realization of this national structure a national movement is necessary. Such a movement should spring spontaneously from the people themselves . . . The present circumstances, however, do not allow us to rely solely on the spontaneous development of such a movement . . . The Government has thus found it necessary to take positive steps for fostering and directing this movement.

The new national structure movement aims at superseding the old party politics predicated upon liberalism . . . Nor can it be allowed to take the form of a single party system . . . as it is contrary to the basic principle of our national policy of 'One Sovereign over all.' In Japan, it is the privilege of every one of His Imperial Majesty's subjects to assist the Throne, and that privilege cannot be monopolized by the power of a single person or a single party.

If there should arise a difference of opinion concerning the assistance to be offered, the final decision would rest with the Throne. And once an Imperial decision has been given, all subjects of the Throne should unite in obeying His Majesty's commands. That is the very essence of Japanese polity.

Briefly, the new national structure is a nation-wide and permanent organization in which the Japanese people in all walks of life are to fulfill their duty of assisting the Throne.

With this announcement, a new organization, the Imperial Rule Assistance Association, was set up. It was soon apparent, however, that this association was not to be a substitute for political party organizations but rather a vehicle for mass mobilization of the people behind Japan's total war effort and a framework within which various agencies could operate to maintain home-front morale. In its activities the I.R.R.A. has sponsored a Youth Corps much like that of the Nazis, and has attempted to co-ordinate the work of the neighborhood associations and the women's patriotic organizations.

For political purposes, there was established in 1942 a subsidiary organization, the Imperial Rule Assistance Political Society, with vague purposes and an ill-defined relationship to the I.R.R.A. This society, however, did provide the means by which Japan's war bosses under Premier Tojo attempted to control elections to the House of Representatives by arranging for nomination of suitable candidates and for support of such candidates among the voters. From all reports it was successful in the 1942 Diet elections, and until Tojo's resignation it attempted to discipline the Diet members in the approved manner of a one-party dictatorship.

Under Premier Koiso the changing leadership of the Imperial Rule Assistance Political Society has reflected a return to political power of professional politicians and representatives of big industrial monopolies who have been fully represented in his Cabinet. In February 1945 an apparent split developed within the society, and the Japanese home radio reported that moves were under way to establish a new single-party structure for the country 'to insure final victory.' From Japanese reports, this split resulted from the irritation of younger politicians and Diet members at control of the society by old-line politicians. A month later, with the usual fanfare, the new totalitarian party, the Imperial Japanese Political Association (*Dai Nippon Seijikai*) was set up to 'insure victory.' Its establishment presaged the fall of the Koiso Cabinet, and its president, General Jiro Minami, who led Japan's invasion of Manchuria, pledged his full support to the new Cabinet of Admiral Baron Suzuki.

The effect of these changes on Japan's political structure remains to be seen, but the political cleavages in Japanese politics in 1945 are the result of military defeats, accelerated bombings of the home islands, and the known failure of their war-production controls to operate efficiently. The industrial monopolists forced Tojo to place control of war production and related matters in the hands of their representatives, and they increased their political power in the government under Koiso. There will undoubtedly be many other changes and not a few Cabinet shake-ups before the war ends, as the various ruling groups within Japan continue their struggles for power in the hope of salvaging something from the defeat which they see drawing closer and closer.

Japan's political party system, used as a tool by the bosses, was discarded by them under the pressures of total war and thus became a war casualty. The end of the war will probably see a revival of old parties and the organization of new ones, but it is certain that unless the power of Japan's bosses is broken, the political parties will again become tools for autocratic control of the people and will remain ineffective instruments for popular control of the government. The Japanese people cannot be expected to develop an interest or a stake in peaceful relations with their neighbors so long as they are denied an effective voice in their government's policies.

If boss rule is broken in Japan, and new political parties and organizations emerge, they will not be able to overcome the past deficiencies in party politics over night. The Japanese will have to learn the responsibilities of citizenship the hard way and bear the cost of many trials and errors, for a period of political experience is a necessary foundation for democratic institutions everywhere. Government *of* the people and *by* the people is a process that must be learned and experienced before government *for* the people can be made to work effectively.

In the interests of a peaceful Japan, and therefore, a peaceful Far East, the United Nations must be prepared to assist the Japanese in removing the barriers to popular control of their government and in enabling them freely to choose more representative leaders so that they can learn to exercise the rights and responsibilities of citizenship. During the period of occupation, the United Nations will automatically give the Japanese a start toward political reconstruction by enforcement of the various measures required for Japan's disarmament and demilitarization. For example, abolition of the army and navy, of the secret police and gendarmerie, and dissolution of the militarist and patriotic societies will severely curtail the activities of those elements in the population that have been most active in repressing the people's rights and most ardent in support of militarism and autocracy.

Also, during the period of occupation, a re-opening of Japan to the outside world, and the institution of the rights of free speech, press, and assembly wherever possible by action of the United Nations authorities will give the Japanese people their first opportunity to begin free discussion of desirable political reforms. In addition, refusal of United Nations officials during occupation to grant authority in Japan to any former member of the Japanese armed forces, to any former militarist or super-patriot, or to any high official who served in Japan's war government since Pearl Harbor might go far to encourage liberal, progressive, and democratic groups to make their programs known and to assume responsibility for carrying out political reforms.

Although there is little disagreement with the policy stated by President Roosevelt that the Japanese 'war-lord form of government' must go, there is a real danger that 'war-lord government' will be narrowly interpreted to mean only a militarist-dominated government and that officials of the United Nations will regard elimination of military leaders from government posts as sufficient guarantee of a peaceful Japan in the future. It is necessary to emphasize again that Japan's 'war-lord government' embraces a whole system of boss rule in which the industrial monopolists, bureaucrats, politicians and the nobility have combined with the militarists in pursuit of aggression and conquest abroad and totalitarianism at home. This boss rule must be eliminated if the Japanese people are ever to have a chance to run their own affairs. It may prove desirable, therefore, as previously indicated, for the United Nations to provide this opportunity by helping to organize a constitutional convention in which the freely elected representatives of the people can draft a 'new political structure' for their nation that will be really new and not just a change of labels, as has been the case so often in the past.[1]

The minimum essentials of constitutional and political reform in Japan would include:

1. Adoption of a new constitution in which the sovereign power of the state is derived from the people, instead of from a theocratic Emperor.

2. A national legislature whose members are elected on the basis of universal suffrage.

3. An executive directly responsible to the elected representatives of the people.

4. Full legislative power over appropriations.

5. Full legislative power to make war and peace and to approve treaties with foreign nations.

6. Separation of the judicial and legislative branches of the government.

7. A bill of civil rights giving full legal protection to the individual citizens against arbitrary acts of government.

---

[1] See previous discussion in Chapters III and VIII.

X

Economic Reconstruction

TOTAL defeat will mean that the Japanese will have to live without benefit of their empire and that whatever economic advantages were derived from their colonies will be lost. Japan will be reduced to the territory with which she began her career as a modern nation, but instead of the thirty or forty million people who inhabited the home islands in 1868, there will be seventy million to care for. The bulk of these seventy million have supported the astonishing growth of Japan's industry and the rapid expansion of her war-machine by their taxes and their cheap labor. But they have been denied the fruits of industrialization and have been deliberately kept poor by the nation's industrial monopolists, who sought profit in foreign trade and armaments. The people of Japan, regimented and poverty-stricken under their ruling classes, have been easily persuaded that conquest and aggression would be worth the sacrifices demanded of them, for they had little to lose. If Japan is to become a peaceful nation after this war, the Japanese people must be given an opportunity to attain an economic stake in the maintenance of peace through development of an economy benefiting the many instead of the few. Only then will promised profits of empire seem less alluring than the effort for a real prosperity at home.

Reconstruction and reform of Japan's economic system are required for the security and peace of Asia, for unless the nation's totalitarian economy is radically altered, economic pressures dammed up in Japan will again lead to empire-building and war. A stable and relatively prosperous Japan can contribute to the economic well-being of all peoples in Asia, but the achievement of these conditions will depend upon the extent to which the economic power of the few can be broken and the poverty of the mass of the people can be alleviated.

Throughout Japan's modern history, her economy has been in the hands of a few industrial monopolies, the huge family combines or *Zaibatsu*. In the early period of industrialization, these family businesses got their start by acting as bankers for the government and by taking over many industries initiated by the state because private capital was lacking. Consequently, these family combines were partners with the government from the beginning and rapidly came to control the wealth of the nation. And from the beginning of Japan's modern period they inevitably exercised a profound influence on both domestic and foreign policy, and grew to be the most important element of the ruling classes from which come the bosses who govern the country.

The names Mitsui and Mitsubishi have become well known in the western world, but altogether there are some fifteen major family monopolies. They consist of numerous corporations and holding companies, usually built around a particular industrial or business activity. The largest of them, however, have become more like vertical trusts with their branches spread through all types of industrial and business enterprise. In most cases, the family control is found in ownership of the principal holding company, while management is in the hands of the best brains the family can buy. The managers are often given a stake in their job through stock ownership in subsidiary companies or marriage within the family.

These fifteen combines control the bulk of both heavy and light industry, either directly or indirectly through their distributing organizations. They control the banking, import and export business, insurance, and shipping. The Mitsui, Mitsubishi, and Sumitomo interests are the largest, and control 25 per cent of the working capital of the nation. These interests, together with the Yasuda, Shibusawa, Kawasaki, Yamaguchi, and Konoike combines, are called by the Japanese the 'big eight'; together they control over 50 per cent of the working capital of Japan. The first five of the 'big eight' hold 40 per cent of the bank deposits, 30 per cent of the business loans, and 40 per cent of the security investments of the nation. The 'lesser seven' include the Momura, Okawa, and Okura family monopolies, with primary interests in banks but controlling many businesses through their subsidiaries, the Ishihara combine of Kobe, the Yamashita fuel and shipping interests, the Asano combine, principally concerned with cement manufacture and shipping, and the Kuhara combine, interested in fuel, steel mills, and electric-machinery manufacturing. The Imperial family is closely associated with these family combines. In addition to an annual Diet appropriation of four and a half million yen for its maintenance, and its ownership of three and a half million acres of valuable forest and prairie land, it profits from the *Zaibatsu* through its holdings of large blocs of stock in most of the important banks and industrial enterprises which they control.

These family combines, the industrial monopolies of Japan, have dictated the economic development of the country. By keeping wages at the lowest possible level, by obtaining higher taxation on land and on agrarian activities than on their own industries, and by supporting enforced savings from the general population, they developed an industrial system based on an increasing export trade designed to provide the necessary imports of raw materials for an expanding heavy industry and armaments program. The low-paid workers, the small merchants, and the poor farmers were not permitted a margin of profit sufficient to buy many of the products of Japan's industries, which in increasing volume flowed into the world market.

It is important to recognize that Japan's war-machine has been built with the assistance of the *Zaibatsu*, whose representatives have never actively opposed the idea of conquest and domination abroad. Rather, the *Zaibatsu* have, in fact, established those economic interests abroad, the protection of which became a major excuse for territorial expansion. They have naturally been conservative in their attitude toward military conquest, opposing methods or policies which seemed to involve too great risk of their profits. Nevertheless, Japan's empire was built by a working combination of the big business combines and the militarists. The *Zaibatsu* have furnished the 'know-how' not only in the manufacture of armaments and munitions for the militarists, but also in the operations of the government. Few Cabinets in Japan have been without representatives of these industrial monopolies, whose managers possess the organizational experience, knowledge of domestic and foreign economic conditions, and the financial astuteness without which the militarists would be helpless.

The *Zaibatsu* helped create and greatly profited by Japan's war machine, but were unable to control the monster they devised. Failing to prevent the militarists from dominating government policies, particularly after 1931, the industrial monopolists joined with the militarists in the attempt to create the Greater East Asia Sphere, where their own stake in successful conquest appeared greater than their chance for profits through peaceful international trade.

The war has not curtailed the influence of the *Zaibatsu*. If anything, it has resulted in a further consolidation of their hold over the economic and political life of the country. The war government of Premier Tojo was largely militarist dominated, and attempts were made to restrict the influence of the industrial monopolists; but the complicated administration of government controls over wages, prices, conditions of labor, and production gradually passed into the hands of representatives of the *Zaibatsu*. The militarists could not manage without them, and the Cabinet of General Koiso, Tojo's successor, again included in the key posts representatives of the great industrial monopolies. Various war controls have resulted in the elimination or merger of many small commercial and industrial enterprises, to the profit of the monopolists, and Japan's war government has increased its participation in banking and business. Key man in Japan's third War Cabinet, headed by Admiral Baron Suzuki, is Admiral Teijiro Toyoda, who has been President of the Japan Steel Works, a Mitsui enterprise, since he left navy service.

In contrast to the wealth and power of the *Zaibatsu*, the Imperial family, and some of the nobility, the people of Japan are poverty-stricken. Few reach the edge of starvation, but most of them live close to the margin of subsistence. Of the country's total area, only 20 per cent can be cultivated, and almost 35 million people must make their living off this arable land, which is hemmed in by rugged mountains and squeezed into valleys and small plains. Japan's population density per square mile of arable land is 2,774, as compared with 2,170 in Britain, 1,709 in Belgium, and 806 in Germany. The average Japanese farm is between 1¼ and 2½ acres, and in 1936 there were 5½ million farm families. Of these families, 7 out of 10 did not own sufficient land for their own use. Approximately half of the arable land was rented by farmers who paid an average of 50 to 60 per cent of their income in rent.

In addition to this high rent, the farmer, as previously indicated, has been forced to pay high taxes in support of expanding industries and increased military expenditures. At the same time, the fertility of the soil has decreased, partly because of deforestation and heavy rains, but mostly because the principal crops he grows—rice, barley, and wheat—have depleted the soil rather than enriched it. So the farmer has had to rely more and more on expensive chemical fertilizer in order to produce good crops. His costs of production have steadily risen, but his income has not. Rather his sources of cash income have been slowly drying up. He could formerly obtain some cash by production of charcoal, but wooded areas have not been adequately replanted and he must go farther and farther from home for the wood he needs, even for his own use. In the past, raising silk cocoons gave him a substantial cash income, but the introduction of rayon, both in Japan and other countries, the demands of an increasing Japanese population for more food, and the expansion of Japan's industries have steadily curtailed both the market for silk and the labor available on the farm for its culture. Formerly, the farmer's son in the army might be able to send home a small allotment from his very low pay, but in recent years the little boxes of ashes sent back to Japan have become more numerous, and there have been fewer allotments.

Japan's farmers live much as they did centuries ago. About the only industrial products in common use are the ten-watt electric bulb, cheap rubber-soled shoes, and cotton cloth. Farmwork is still largely hand labor with primitive tools, in which the whole family must join. The rural population has been steadily increasing and the farmer has had more mouths to feed. In a year of poor crops or low prices he is often forced to sell his daughters to the city brothel or to the labor contractors for the city factories, in order to obtain a little extra cash to pay off part of his debts. The net result of this farm poverty is to sink Japan's agrarian population deeper and deeper into debt, since money must be borrowed for taxes, for seed for next year's crop, and even for food for the family. Between 1914 and 1937, the total debt of the nation's farmers increased over four times, and the burden is growing steadily.

During the war the farmer has been urged to raise more and more food, but the costs of seed, fertilizer, and other essentials has steadily risen, while the prices he gets for his crops have lagged behind. Rising taxes and enforced savings have increased his indebtedness, and the demands of the military services and of war industries for more laborers have deprived him of the help of his sons and daughters who used to work in his fields.

The lot of the industrial worker and the small merchant in the larger towns and cities has been little better than that of the farmer. Their living conditions are still primitive, and modern conveniences are unknown except to the well-to-do. Like the farmer, the worker and small merchant must labor long hours to earn enough for the bare essentials of food, shelter, and clothing. The small merchant who has converted his little shop to war production has had any increased profits he received eaten up by higher taxes, enforced war savings, and the higher prices he pays for manufacturing materials, for less nourishing food, and for shoddy clothing. While Japan's workers in war industries are making higher wages, war prices and taxes plus longer working hours have resulted in little relative improvement over their pre-war lot.

Inevitably the end of the war will find the Japanese poorer than at any time in their modern history. All of the conditions which have in the past operated to keep them poor will have been accentuated by the war. Reconversion of war industries to peace-time production and the demobilization of the armed forces will produce a severe problem of unemployment. Loss of the war will throw Japan's economy out of gear, and only the most drastic readjustments in the economic structure can succeed in developing a postwar economy in which the masses of the people can at last be given an opportunity to achieve some degree of economic security.

In considering the results of total defeat on Japan's economic system, the question most often asked is whether the Japanese, having lost the war and lost their empire, can develop a healthy, stable economy based on their home islands, which will provide their people with a rising standard of living. Any answer to the question, 'Can the Japanese survive without empire?' must necessarily be based on an estimate of Japan's economic liabilities and assets after defeat.

When the war ends, the Japanese will face many liabilities, which will have to be overcome in some degree if economic recovery is to be achieved within a reasonable time. Their principal liabilities will include:

A physical debilitation of the population due to improper diet and lack of sufficient medical care;

War casualties, said to have reached over two and a half million in 1944;

An undetermined number of demobilized soldiers and sailors who must be absorbed into industry or agriculture and who may demand pensions or other forms of compensation for their war services;

An unpredictable number of Japanese civilians, perhaps as many as two million, who will be repatriated to Japan from various parts of the 'co-prosperity sphere';

Loss of overseas possessions from which valuable raw materials have been easily obtained in the past;

Loss of foreign markets, business connections abroad, and valuable assets outside of Japan which may be confiscated by the United Nations;

A staggering war debt (for Japan) and the problem of adjusting internal finances in accord with radically changed economic conditions;

Restrictions and penalties imposed by the United Nations in the form of reparations and/or economic controls;

Industrial re-conversion to peace-time production—a task which cannot adequately be planned in advance of defeat;

An unpredictable amount of destruction of industrial plant, equipment, transport, and housing as a result of hostilities;

Loss of good-will abroad with resulting barriers to Japanese foreign trade and business that may be continued and extended.

Against all these liabilities and others now unforeseen, there must be balanced certain economic assets which the Japanese will possess after defeat. The most important of these assets will include:

A large population, trained to obedience and to regard frugal living as a matter of pride;

A corps of skilled technicians and industrial workers;

A high rate of literacy and the best system of technical education in the Far East;

A high level of managerial skill, organizational experience, and knowledge of modern business and financial operations;

Relief from supporting the uneconomic burden of armaments and maintenance of large armed forces;

A well-developed system of home or 'cottage' industries suited to production of a wide range of consumers' goods;

Whatever industrial plant, equipment, transport, and other materials remain intact after hostilities;

War experience in the development of substitute products and synthetics;

A considerable hydro-electric power potential which can partially offset deficiencies in coal;

A relative self-sufficiency in food resources capable of more efficient development;

A geographic location close to potential markets in Asia in which Japanese goods can compete favorably under most conditions.

In the past, Japan has utilized her economic and other assets in building an empire and thus has reduced her economic liabilities, but this has been done at the expense of her own people and of other peoples whom she has dominated. The consequences of this policy have been war and suffering. Japan's problem after defeat will be similar to that of the past: to devise means of overcoming her liabilities and utilizing her assets to the best advantage. The choice before Japan is clear. Lacking the resources of a great power, the Japanese can either choose to follow the old road of empire-building in the hope of re-attaining great power rank, or they can choose to accept the status of a middle-class power commensurate with the assets they will possess in their home islands after defeat. The first choice will mean continued poverty at home and will inevitably lead again to war and suffering. The second choice can result in the development of a peaceful, prosperous Japan, giving to the Japanese people a better life than they have ever known.

It is essential to the security of the United Nations and to the peace of the world that the Japanese be persuaded to make this second choice, to accept the status of a middle-class power, and to recognize that they have more to gain for themselves in the role of an Asiatic Sweden than they can ever gain by attempting to revive their past imperialist role without the resources to maintain it and with the certain risks of another war and another defeat if they attempt it.

The choice for the Japanese will be easier in some respects because Japan will be reduced in fact to the status of a middle-class power as a result of her defeat when the United Nations take away her empire and complete her disarmament. By disarmament alone the United Nations will confer an economic advantage upon the Japanese that will enable them to reorganize their economic system without having to bear the heavy and uneconomic burden of armaments and the support of armed forces. And by the restrictions imposed upon Japan in the postwar period to prevent her rearmament, the Japanese will be forced to consider a new economic role for their nation in accord with their changed status.

On the other hand, the greatest obstacle to Japanese acceptance of this new role is the fact that Japan can only prosper as a middle-class power when the stranglehold of the *Zaibatsu* and their supporters on the nation's economy is broken and when those fundamental economic reforms are undertaken which will give to the Japanese people a chance to make a decent living for themselves. It is certain that the industrial monopolists will resist every effort to deprive them of their economic power and political influence. Fortunately it is also certain that this domination of Japan's wealth by the few has been deeply resented by large elements in the population. In the past this resentment has found expression in rice riots, struggles of the farmers to gain relief from high taxes, high rents, and high interest rates, and in industrial strikes by workers desiring better wages, hours, and conditions of work. But popular dissatisfaction with economic conditions has always been suppressed and channeled into support for expanding conquests by co-operation between the *Zaibatsu* and the militarists, who, with the bureaucrats and politicians, have had a common interest in maintaining their power over the Japanese people. Economic reform will be impossible until the concentrated power of these bosses has been broken.

If the Japanese, with the assistance of the United Nations, undertake the political reforms necessary to the transfer of power from the hands of the ruling groups to the chosen representatives of the people, then the development of an economy directed toward the advancement of the whole Japanese people will be possible. United Nations assistance in political reform within Japan, therefore, will constitute an important aid to the inauguration of economic reforms. Although the direction of Japan's postwar economy will depend largely upon United Nations actions respecting such matters as tariffs, currency stabilization, access to raw materials, migration, and related problems, the broad outline of economic reforms designed to transform Japan into a relatively prosperous middle-class power can be set forth. These reforms would be directed at achieving a large expansion in products for home consumption, a more rational balance between agriculture and industry, and the export of those commodities which could be profitably sold abroad without state subsidy.

Some of the principal reform measures proposed in the many economic surveys of Japan made by both Japanese and foreign experts include:

1. Expansion of light industries for increased production of such items as chemicals, hardware, tools, small machines, electrical appliances, clothing, household equipment, small farm tools, and light farm machinery.

2. Progressive introduction of higher wages, shorter working hours, and better working conditions in industry in line with the conventions and recommendations of the International Labor Organization.

3. Decentralization of economic power by removal of control of working capital from the industrial monopolies, and by taxation and abolition of holding companies and subsidies, so as to provide opportunities for profitable operation of an increasing number of small business enterprises.

4. Development of home or 'cottage' industries under regulation or on the co-operative principle, utilizing the experience of the Chinese Industrial Co-operatives.

5. Reorganization of the system of taxation so as to distribute the tax burden more evenly between agriculture and industry.

6. Re-adjustment of farm holdings so as to reduce farm tenancy, combined with a reduction of farm indebtedness through a moratorium or by partial or complete cancellation.

7. Expansion of rural credit facilities, reduction of interest

rates on farm borrowing, and consolidation of marketing and distribution facilities in the rural areas.

8. Development of crop diversification, particularly cover crops, combined with expansion of cattle and sheep raising on the higher uplands, both to increase food resources and provide more animal fertilizer.

9. Development of national and local planning agencies with trained personnel, to co-ordinate reforms and to provide for an orderly economic development.

XI

Social Reconstruction

A RECONSTRUCTION of Japanese society and a renovation of the underlying philosophy, customs, and traditions of the Japanese people must accompany political and economic reforms. For if the Japanese people hold fast to their old ways of life, to their ideas of race-superiority, emperor worship, and belief in their divine mission to rule the world, political and economic reforms will soon be smothered in new outbursts of excessive nationalism.

Japan's rigid social structure has provided the perfect framework within which her war-lords and her industrial monopolists have been able to mould the ideas and beliefs of the Japanese people in the close confines of a super-patriotism and a ruthless nationalism. The customs and traditions that regulate Japanese society and that have been perpetuated to serve the demands of autocratic rule stem from a feudalism overlaid with mystical beliefs and a religious-nationalistic fanaticism revolving around the position and authority of the Imperial Throne. This archaic society must give way to changes which will permit the Japanese people to develop that respect for other peoples and civilizations which is the essence of peaceful international relations.

Foreigners are usually impressed by the extreme courtesy of the Japanese, by the picturesqueness of their customs and modes of living, and by their apparently modern industrial system. Foreigners see the beautiful temples, witness the Kabuki or Noh dramas, the tea ceremony and the colorful festivals. They see the farmer and his family at work in the fields, the fisherman along the shore, and the workers in the cities. They see evidence of industrial civilization in the city buildings, transport systems, and large factories. To the visitor, the Japanese seem a happy, industrious, and contented people.

Few foreigners take the time to probe into the beliefs and ideas behind the customary courtesies, the festivals and rituals. Few foreigners leave the beaten tourist paths to observe how the masses of the people live in the crowded countryside or the city slums, or to enquire into the essential facts of mass living standards. As a result, many past visitors to Japan have found it hard to believe that a people possessing obvious artistic talents, seemingly courteous, contented, and industrious, could exhibit the shocking brutalities of a savage militarism. The casual visitor to Japan has seen a peaceful-appearing nation. The realities of Japanese life are very different.

Japanese life is insecure. The grinding poverty to which the Japanese have been subjected has left only the barest margin between subsistence and starvation. The benefits of industrialism and empire-building have been reserved for the few at the top of the economic structure. Struggle against economic insecurity has been the common lot of the people in Japan from feudal times to the present. Whether in the cities or on the farms, for the bulk of the population the business of making a living consumes the energies of the whole family. A sudden fall in prices of farm products, a change in world market conditions, or the commercial manipulations of the economic over-lords can easily wipe out the small margin of profit permitted the people under the best circumstances.

The struggle to live is made more difficult by the recurrence of natural disasters. The mountainous character of the country and the nature of the climate make damage by wind, rain, floods, or drought a constant threat to the crops upon which half of the people depend for a living. In the towns and cities widespread wooden construction of homes and buildings makes fire an ever-present danger in the absence of adequate water systems and efficient fire-fighting equipment. Hardly a month passes by without record of serious earthquake shocks, and the great disaster of 1923 is still fresh in the minds of most Japanese. Earthquakes are often accompanied by tidal waves that inundate the productive lowlands along the shore, and damaging typhoons are a semi-annual occurrence. The yearly losses of life and property from fire, floods, and similar disasters add considerably to the burdens of the people and have created a sense of physical insecurity which is the more demoralizing since these natural disasters cannot be fully overcome by human means.

To this struggle of the Japanese people against economic and physical insecurity must be added the feeling of insecurity resulting from Japanese conquest and aggression. Five wars in half a century have left the Japanese people with no prolonged periods of peace in their modern history. Promised profits from expanding conquests in Asia have always been held out as a lure for the people to make their sacrifice at home 'to assist the Emperor in fulfilling the injunctions of the divine ancestors.' Since the Manchurian invasion, Japan's leaders have held the nation in an almost constant state of crisis. The people have been called upon to mobilize 'their spiritual and material resources' by harder work, longer hours, and greater sacrifices, so that their empire might 'surmount the dangers ahead.' This pressure from above, keying the people to a pitch of emotional fervor, while at the same time warning them of threats to their existence as a nation, has made most Japanese willing supporters of empire-building as an eventual means of overcoming the insecurities of their life at home. Freedom from fear and freedom from want are coveted by the Japanese, but they have been aspirations perverted to gain support for the imperialistic policies of their war-lords.

The insecurities of life to which they have been subjected and which they keenly feel have made the Japanese people more amenable to the regulation of rigid customs in a society controlled by the few. In no other modern nation have ancient and primitive habits and ways of doing things been so tenaciously preserved. Almost every act of the Japanese from birth to death is regulated by customs and traditions closely linked to Buddhism, to Shintoism, and to local superstitions and ceremonies. Custom regulates the eating habits, the dress, the construction of houses and arrangements of rooms, the modes of speech, and the personal and family relations of the Japanese to a minute degree. Custom has fixed the status of women as obedient daughters to their fathers and as servants to their husbands. Custom and tradition give a high place in Japanese society to the soldier and sailor who are privileged to fulfil the direct orders of the divine emperor, the 'father' of the Japanese people.

The local festivals of the villages and towns, the worship of numerous local deities, or *kami*, the ceremonies of the Buddhist temples and Shinto shrines, the celebration of local and national holidays, the perpetuation of ancient superstitions combine to make the Japanese continually aware of the importance of custom and tradition in their daily life. Many Japanese cannot explain why they do certain things a certain way or continue habits that seem out of place in a modern world, except to say 'it is *shukan*, custom.' This is sufficient explanation in a society in which the expression of individual tastes and desires brings social ostracism. Living in close physical association with each other, and engaged in a common struggle against the insecurities of life, the Japanese have come to depend upon conformity to custom as a means of attaining some sense of stability in an otherwise unstable existence. Retreat into the theatrical, mystical world of ancient beliefs, religious rituals, festivals, and superstitions is a major method of making the hard realities of life bearable for the mass of the people.

This rigid social system has been consciously kept alive and actively perpetuated by Japan's ruling groups to keep the people amenable to their will and to prevent a successful challenge to their power and profits. Ancient beliefs, religious practices, and old superstitions have been interwoven with national patriotism by Japan's real rulers to obtain mass support for their autocratic control at home and their imperialism abroad. It is hard to differentiate between customs and rituals that are the outgrowth of primitive beliefs and later religious development, and those ideas and ceremonies inspired by nationalism. Japanese primitive superstitions, native Shintoism, Buddhism, and nationalism have been combined as a basis for Japan's regulated society.

It is remarkable testimony to the astuteness of Japan's aristocratic oligarchy of the late nineteenth century that it was able to effect a transition from a feudal society to an industrialized state with so little change in the customs and traditions of old Japan. But this was done deliberately, both as a means of maintaining rigid control over the lives of the people and of constructing a nationalism uniquely Japanese in character. It was not done without opposition, but so strong has been the grip of Japan's real rulers on the national life that they have been able to suppress any concerted moves for social change and to smother any widespread acceptance of non-Japanese ideas.

The ruling oligarchy that took Japan into the modern world was successful in preserving the old customs and ways of life largely by controlling the educational system. Formal, compulsory education was introduced in Japan in 1872 as a state enterprise. The educational system was based upon a study of American and European practices, many of which were adapted to Japanese needs. It was developed at a time when the Japanese were borrowing heavily from western civilization those forms and techniques judged necessary to their rapid industrialization and to the expansion of their armed forces. These changes naturally resulted in the introduction of many western ideas at variance with Japanese ways and beliefs. The ruling oligarchy, therefore, sought to prevent the spread of liberal ideas, western individualism, and non-Japanese beliefs by a revival of old traditions and the inculcation of patriotism and emperor-loyalty through the school system.

The ruling oligarchy, thoroughly nationalistic, obtained a powerful sanction for these aims in the Imperial Rescript on Education, issued on October 30, 1890. Regarded by many as a document fully as important as the Constitution, it was drafted by Akimasa Yoshikawa, then Minister of Education, who admitted that its chief purpose was to halt the spread of foreign ideas within the country. Through interpretation it has been made the source and sanction of a nationalistic, regimented educational system. Its text reads as follows:

Know ye Our subjects:

Our Imperial Ancestors have founded our Empire on a basis broad and everlasting and have deeply and firmly implanted virtue; Our subjects, ever united in loyalty and filial piety, have from generation to generation illustrated the beauty thereof. This is the glory of the fundamental character of Our Empire and herein also lies the source of Our education. Ye, Our subjects, be filial to your parents, affectionate to your brothers and sisters; as husbands and wives be harmonious, as friends true; bear yourselves in modesty and moderation; extend your benevolence to all; pursue learning and cultivate arts, and thereby develop your intellectual faculties and perfect your moral powers; furthermore advance the public good and promote common interests; always respect the Constitution and observe the laws; should any emergency arise, offer yourself courageously to the State; and thus guard and maintain the prosperity of Our Imperial Throne, coeval with heaven and earth. So shall ye not only be Our good and faithful subjects, but render illustrious the best traditions of your forefathers.

The way here set forth is indeed the teaching bequeathed by Our Imperial Ancestors, to be observed alike by their descendants and subjects, infallible for all ages and true in all places. It is Our wish to lay to heart in all reverence, in common with you Our subjects, that we may thus attain the same virtue.

The 30th day of the tenth month of the 23rd year of Meiji.
(Imperial Sign Manual)   (Imperial Seal)

Many of the virtues urged in this rescript are acceptable by western standards. There can be little quarrel with efforts to induce people to exhibit qualities of moderation, modesty, and benevolence, or to lead them to develop their intellectual faculties, to become law-abiding, or to offer their lives to their nation in time of emergency. However, a close reading of the Rescript shows that it can be easily interpreted to support the concept that the individual exists for the state, 'to guard and maintain the prosperity of Our Imperial Throne.' This, in fact, has been its interpretation in the hands of Japan's nationalists and their interpretation has been forced upon the people as 'indeed the teaching bequeathed by Our Imperial Ancestors, to be observed alike by descendants and subjects, *infallible for all ages and true in all places.*' [1] Any attempt, therefore, to give a more liberal interpretation to this charter of the educational system has met with the charge of disloyalty to the Emperor, whose position and authority must never be questioned. Tatsuo Kawai, Japanese Foreign

---

[1] Author's italics.

Office Spokesman at the beginning of Japan's war with China in 1937, has written that,

While the Constitution provided a well-elaborated modern system of government of the Occidental type, the Imperial Rescript on Education was intended to elucidate the eternal virtues of old Japan. Exhorting the nation to loyalty, patriotism and solidarity, the Rescript put a healthy check upon overzealous campaigners for 'liberty and equality.'

The way was prepared for a nationalistic education system a year before the promulgation of the Imperial Rescript, when orders were issued banning all strictly religious teaching, whether Buddhist or Christian, in the public schools. At the same time the government ordered compulsory instruction in the principles of loyalty to the Emperor and patriotism, two hours per week in all schools up to the universities. In the higher educational institutions the students receive compulsory instruction in *kokumin dotoku*, literally, 'national morality,' as part of their regular course. School books for all grades, including the universities, became more and more nationalistic in character, extolling the 'imperial line unbroken for ages eternal,' the virtues of the 'true' Imperial Way, and the duty of absolute loyalty and obedience to the Emperor. Histories repeated the myths of national origin to give them the flavor of authentic facts. The distinctive qualities of Japanese art, language, and customs were emphasized, not only as 'unique' but also as the only salvation for other nations which possessed no Imperial Ancestors to guide their destinies. To these 'unique' characteristics have been added a 'Japanese science' and a 'Japanese inventive genius,' which, combined with the greatly 'superior quality of the Japanese spirit,' have been used to glorify the state and to demonstrate its superiority to all other nations.

Beginning with the Meji period, the Ministry of Education

exercised the most careful surveillance over teachers. Any who failed to observe absolute loyalty to the Emperor, to teach this virtue to their students, or who allowed any taint of the 'dangerous thoughts' of modernism or liberalism to enter into their teaching have been severely censored or have lost their jobs.

Students are fed the host of carefully approved ideas and facts selected by the nationalists. From the early grades through the universities, free expression of thought has been suppressed and classroom instruction has been barren of any exchange of ideas in a search for truth, for the 'truth' in Japan is only what the 'infallible' Throne approves as interpreted by the ruling coalition. Not many students go beyond the compulsory six years of elementary school. Still fewer go on from the middle schools to colleges and universities, and those who do find the emphasis placed on the acquisition of practical skills and training.

The mass of Japan's literate population have never been exposed to non-Japanese ideas or to adequate knowledge of other peoples and civilizations. They can read, but only what is permitted by Japan's rulers to serve the ends of their regimented society. The Japanese people are ignorant of the common currency of western thought which emphasizes individual rights in society, the intrinsic worth of the individual, and the concept that the state exists for the people and not the reverse, as the Japanese are constantly taught. It is no wonder, then, that in more than half a century under this Japanese educational system there has been bred a nation of fanatics, a people who, when confronted by facts or evidence contrary to what they have been told or taught, resort to the fanatic's defense, 'You don't understand our true spirit, your criticism is insincere.'

Of prime importance is the fact that Japan's educational system has been used from the start as a gigantic pre-induction training program to provide the soldiery for her mass armies. Universal conscription was introduced in 1873 and all male Japanese must serve a three-year term. From the primary grades through the universities, the boys are prepared for army service and thoroughly indoctrinated with a martial spirit based upon the belief that death for the god-Emperor is the highest glory the soldier or sailor can achieve. Beginning in the primary grades, Japanese boys are required to wear a semi-military uniform. They learn to drill, to use guns, and to harden themselves by long endurance marches in all kinds of weather; fencing and knife-throwing, wrestling and all sports that have a martial origin or use are encouraged. The military history of their country is drilled into them and military heroes are made their idols through regular ceremonies and pilgrimages to the great shrines and monuments commemorating war-like deeds.

When at eighteen the conscript is ready to enter the army, his early schooling has made him familiar with the rudiments of military training and his frugal living has inured him to hardship. But more important, he has absorbed in his formative years the concepts of absolute obedience to his superiors, unquestioned loyalty to his Emperor's commands, and firm belief in the destiny of Japan as a dominant nation. These ideas have been kept alive in him not only through the schools, but also by means of the activities and propaganda of the ex-service men's associations and the patriotic societies whose membership is spread throughout the population; most families include an ex-sailor or an ex-soldier in addition to the school boys who are being prepared for service.

Since early 1944, the school system has been completely subordinated to the war effort, and the attitude of Japanese leaders, as expressed in public statements, has been to disregard the educational needs of the nation except in so far as the schools contribute to military training or to the rapid replenishment of the country's skilled labor force.

Increasing numbers of teachers have been drafted into the army or have been forced to work in war industries, without adequate replacements provided for except in technical schools. School buildings have been taken over by the government to house war workers or as hospitals and warehouses. An increasing number of schools have been partially converted to factories by installation of simple machinery at which the school children are employed from a half to two-thirds of the time normally devoted to school work. All of the technical schools are operated on this basis and contribute not only to the training of skilled workers but also to the actual production of war materials.

Japanese home broadcasts have been urging youngsters from twelve years of age up to 'volunteer' for war work either in a factory or on a farm, and the military services are reported to have begun accepting fourteen- and fifteen-year-olds for training. The labor draft law which was made effective in 1944 provides for registration of all males from twelve to sixty years of age and all females between twelve and forty years of age. The government is empowered to send these labor conscripts anywhere they are considered necessary. For the past two years, school children have been virtually forced to work on the farms and in the cultivation of vacant land in or near the towns and cities, for which they have been given school credit. A low wage is paid them for their labor, which undoubtedly has been the chief reason for lack of vigorous public objection, since the families of the children need whatever extra cash can be earned.

After the first devastating incendiary bomb raids on Tokyo, Kobe, and other Japanese cities in early March 1945, the Japanese Cabinet had passed by an emergency session of the Diet a law empowering the army to confiscate any or all 'land, buildings, and materials' in the country for defense purposes and to assign summarily any or all citizens to 'military works.' With this act Japan was placed under virtual martial law and the whole citizenry subordinated to a last-ditch defence of their homeland. On March 18, the Cabinet announced that all schools, colleges, and universities would be closed for one year beginning April 1, 1945. Only first-grade classes in the primary schools are to be continued, thus releasing all children over six years old and their teachers for war work. As with Japan's political parties, the educational system has become a wartime casualty.

The breakdown of Japan's educational system in some respects may prove advantageous for the postwar period, since it may make easier a thorough overhauling of the whole educational structure, its methods and objectives. With war pressures removed and the use of the schools for military training prohibited, liberal Japanese leaders at last may have an opportunity to introduce long-overdue reforms in education, which, if carried through successfully, would do a great deal to change the old patterns of society.

One reform that has long been urged by a few Japanese and by many foreigners is an expansion of the educational opportunities for women in Japan so that their chance for learning may be equal to that offered the men. Up to the present time, women's education has been limited to the lower grades and the standards for girls' schools are admittedly less strict than those for boys. Although the government early established a system of technical schools, colleges, and universities for men, no such institutions have been provided for women, and those who can afford higher education must rely on less than a dozen private colleges, most of them established under the auspices of foreign missionaries.

Providing educational opportunities for Japanese women might be the best method of eradicating one aspect of

Japan's rigid social system, which has marked Japanese society as feudal and has made maintenance of rigid social controls by the nation's bosses easier. Women have always had an inferior status in Japanese society and the feudal concept has prevailed in all classes that women's place is 'to minister to man's needs, subscribe with blind faith to his ideas, obey his commands, and give him children.' Custom, tradition, and rules of etiquette have bound women to this status of servitude as rigidly as any laws.

The girl is taught to obey her parents implicitly and, except in certain sections of middle-class and wealthy Japanese society, must accept the husband chosen for her by her parents. With little chance of meeting boys of her own age during her youth, she has no opportunity to become acquainted with her prospective husband before marriage. The two families involved usually make the marriage arrangements, with the objective of enhancing their wealth or social prestige. Once married, the girl must obey her husband in all things and may divorce him only in the most extreme circumstances. The man, on the other hand, has as much freedom as he desires and can divorce his wife and retain custody of their children with little difficulty. A widowed woman, by custom, must conform to the dictates of her son or her husband's parents.

This inferior status of women in Japan has made it easier for the ruling groups to maintain their social controls, to preserve archaic customs and traditions, and to spread their nationalistic doctrines. Japanese women know little beyond the traditional ideas and customs they have been taught at an early age, and their consequent urge to remain conformists exercises a restraining influence on any men in their family who wish to break with the past. If the position of women in postwar Japan can be altered, the base for much of the old social system can be eliminated and new values and standards will have a better chance to gain acceptance.

In China, as well as in other Oriental countries, the gradual emancipation of women has been a sure indication that social change was taking place and that modern ideas and beliefs were gaining ground. Once the old social restraints in Japan are modified or removed altogether, Japanese women may be able to mobilize their talents in the fields of political, social, and economic reforms and help to initiate and to carry through changes at a much more rapid pace than now seems possible. Indeed, the emancipation of Japanese women from their inferior status will be a certain indication that fundamental social reforms are taking place within Japan and that the old social system is giving way to one more in keeping with the modern world. Such a change, when it comes, will also mean that the traditional and nationalistic appeals of Japan's old ruling groups will have less validity and will make far more difficult any attempts to gain support for future aggression.

Changing Japan from a warlike to a peaceful nation, in the final analysis will involve the re-education of the whole nation. The Japanese have been taught to believe in their absolute superiority to other peoples and their unquestioned right to dominate Asia. They have been taught that their Emperor is divine and that they are endowed as a race with special and superhuman attributes not found in any other nations. They must undergo a process of re-education in which they learn to appreciate the ideas and culture of their neighbors. They must be given the opportunity to test their own ideas against those of other peoples, to measure their customs and traditions by the standards of other civilizations, and to subject their ancient myths and legends to the investigations of historical scholarship. Only by such means can the Japanese see their national institutions in true perspective and develop those elements of their national culture in which they and other peoples can share a legitimate pride.

Such re-education is essential to a peaceful Japan in the future and it is basically a task that the Japanese must undertake themselves. The task will be slow and difficult, for remnants of the old ruling groups will still remain in Japan and will be opposed to change. There will be an inevitable tendency to accept reforms by decree, to take the bare skeleton for the substance. Freed from old restraints, many Japanese will not know where to start or where to stop, what ideas and institutions to accept, and what to reject. Many will resent offers of assistance or advice from the outside as unwarranted interference in their internal affairs. Many others will be quick to promote superficial changes acceptable to the United Nations in the hope that such window-dressing will aid their nation in re-establishing its status as a full member of the international community.

The Japanese can be aided in the process of re-education, however, if the United Nations take the necessary measures to reopen Japan to the outside world as soon as possible after her defeat, and during the period of occupation. Since 1931, the Japanese have been increasingly cut off from the information and knowledge of the rest of the world. Since Pearl Harbor, they have been fed only the pre-digested news and information that their bosses desired them to have. If they are ever to set about the task of learning the facts of international life, Japan must be reopened to unrestricted contact with other nations and to uncensored access to the world's knowledge. The reopening of Japan is a responsibility that the United Nations must undertake during the period of occupation. This process will be assisted initially by United Nation's policies and actions designed primarily to disarm and to demilitarize Japan. Elimination of the army and navy, of the secret police and gendarmarie, dissolution of the militarist and patriotic societies and the trial and punishment of Japanese war criminals are measures which will remove many of the elements most repressive in the past of Japan's freedom of intercourse with the outside world.

The reconstruction of Japanese society will involve both internal reforms, which the Japanese themselves must undertake, and policies and actions by the United Nations to assist the Japanese in the process. Minimum reforms in the social field should include:

1. Reopening all channels of communication with the outside world and promoting cultural exchanges of every sort with the United Nations.

2. Maintenance of freedom of religion, press, speech, and assembly.

3. Reorganization of the Japanese educational system, including elimination of indoctrination in state Shinto and any type of military training or militarist teaching.

4. Encouragement of organizations through which Japanese can collectively voice their grievances and express their opinions; these would include labor unions, farmer's organizations, tenant's and small merchants' associations.

5. Encouragement of private organizations for study and dissemination of knowledge of other peoples, their culture and institutions.

6. Granting to women equal legal rights with men, as a first step, along with universal suffrage, toward changing their inferior status in society.

XII

The Future of Japan

JAPAN will enter the postwar world a defeated and a disarmed
nation, stripped of her empire and reduced to the status of a
second-rate power. She will be a much weaker nation in defeat than was Germany in 1919, and for this reason there are
many who believe that she will be unable to launch a new
aggression for generations and that the United Nations, therefore, need not be concerned with political, economic, or social reforms in Japan after the war. Such an assertion is based
upon a number of dangerous assumptions which, if accepted,
would seriously jeopardize the ultimate objective of the
United Nations—the development of a peaceful and a trustworthy Japan.

First, it is dangerous to assume that a greatly weakened
but essentially unreformed Japan will not again become a
trouble-maker in the Far East and eventually renew her bid
for empire. Without fundamental changes in Japan's political,
economic, and social structure, representatives of the old ruling groups will retain their power, and opportunity will be
provided for the militarists and their civilian collaborators to
work from behind the scenes in planning to revenge their defeat. It is certain that these old ruling groups, if left relatively
undisturbed, will make every effort to appear subservient to
the demands of the United Nations. It is likely that they will
go through the motions of initiating those reforms which will
lead the United Nations to believe that the Japanese have
learned the lesson that aggression does not pay. It is certain
that they will make every effort to conceal their nation's real

strength and their own imperialist aims, while endeavoring
to demonstrate their country's peaceful intentions, just as
they did before Pearl Harbor. Their object would be to gain
release from onerous peace terms as soon as possible. But if
the old order remains in Japan after defeat, the old ruling
groups will look to the re-creation of the Greater East Asia
Co-Prosperity Sphere as the best means of keeping their people united behind them and as the only means of retaining
their influence, their power, and their profits. They will use
all the methods of political maneuver and economic penetra-
tion in which they have shown themselves so adept in the
past.

Second, it is dangerous to assume that the defeat of Japan
will wipe out all Japanese influence and prestige in the rest
of Asia. While it is true that Japanese conquest has left bitterness and hatred in its wake, the Japanese may well retain
a core of influence among the peoples of the 'co-prosperity
sphere,' even after defeat. Much will depend upon the policies
of the returning colonial powers in southeast Asia and on the
ability of the United Nations generally to reconstruct the
economy of the Pacific area in a reasonable length of time.
But unless the United Nations can offer the peoples of Asia
concrete evidence that their welfare will be given first consideration by the United Nations in their postwar Far Eastern policies, then Japanese propaganda will again take effect.
The Japanese will certainly exploit to their own advantage
any dissatisfaction the Asiatic people feel with their lot in the
postwar period. The Japanese have posed as the champions
of Asiatic freedom against western imperialism, and to the
degree that any group of people in Asia believe that this imperialism has returned unabated after the war, Japanese influence will profit.

Third, it is dangerous to assume that maintenance of order
and stability in Japan immediately after the war by reliance

on representatives of the old ruling groups—the industrial monopolists, the bankers, bureaucrats, or politicians—is more desirable than risking a period of instability during which new, liberal, and democratic groups are given an opportunity to establish themselves and begin the tasks of reform. It is certain that members of the old ruling coalition will bid for United Nations recognition as the only group capable of maintaining peace and order within their country, and it is equally certain that they will oppose fundamental democratic reforms as they have done in the past. For the United Nations to compromise their ultimate goal of a reformed and peaceful Japan by acceptance of the assumed short-term advantages of immediate postwar stability under the old ruling groups would be not only a denial of their war aim to crush Japanese militarism but also a sure guarantee of future Japanese aggression.

Fourth, it is dangerous to assume that it will be easy for the United Nations to remain united in their determination to police Japan. Eventually there will be the danger that home-front weariness, distasteful squabbles, and divergent interests will lead to a relaxation of controls by the United Nations, and the all-too-familiar story of Germany will be repeated. But indefinite policing of Japan will be required if the United Nations are unwilling to assist the Japanese in accepting their new status as a middle-class power, for otherwise an unreformed Japan will be only too anxious to use every stratagem to gain release from restrictions upon her freedom of action in order to restore her prestige as a great power and inevitably to attempt the re-building of her empire.

The only alternative to the risks of war inherent in action based on any of the assumptions just described is the development of a United Nations policy that will combine the restrictions and controls necessary for prevention of Japanese rearmament with constructive measures designed to assist the

Japanese in developing a stake in the maintenance of peace. A comprehensive policy to this end has been suggested in the preceding chapters dealing with specific problems of Japan's future and is summarized below. Many of the policies and actions proposed will be automatically invoked by United Nations authorities during the period of occupation as essential to military government of Japan. How far these and additional measures are to be pursued beyond the immediate period of military occupation is a question on which general public opinion may be decisive.

A satisfactory United Nations policy toward Japan will provide, first of all, that complete and unconditional surrender by the Japanese shall involve approval of the terms of peace by all Japan's highest authorities, including the Emperor, as a means of fixing responsibility for Japan's aggression. The United Nations should occupy Japan to whatever extent and for whatever length of time is necessary for total disarmament, for adequately demonstrating to the Japanese people the fact of their defeat, and for the purpose of helping to initiate those minimum changes required to start Japan on the road to a peaceful future.

The United Nations should insist on complete Japanese disarmament; elimination of the army and navy; dissolution of all militarist and patriotic societies, the secret police, and gendarmerie; and the trial and punishment of war criminals. The United Nations should prohibit rearmament in any form and set up a Control Commission to enforce this prohibition. Such a Commission should have powers of inspection within Japan and should be required to render annual, public reports of its investigations. As additional safeguards against rearmament, the United Nations should prohibit all airplane construction, the importation and production of light metals needed for such construction, and should limit Japan's postwar merchant-ship tonnage to approximately three million tons, an amount sufficient for her coastwise Asiatic trade. These restrictions on Japan's freedom should be continued until such time as there is satisfactory proof that the Japanese have renounced their imperialist ambitions.

To promote the development of a peaceful and trustworthy Japan, the United Nations should refuse to give authority to any militarists or to civilians who have held responsible posts since Pearl Harbor. The United Nations should 'use' the Emperor solely for the purpose of documenting defeat and should in no way give support to the maintenance of the institution of the Imperial Throne. Constructively, the United Nations should aid and support those Japanese groups willing to undertake the difficult tasks of reforming an autocratic government into a popularly controlled political system, of breaking the power of the industrial monopolists— the *Zaibatsu*—and introducing changes in the economy to advance the welfare of the whole people, and of ridding their nation of its feudal, militaristic traditions and institutions. As a first step in this direction, the United Nations may find it necessary or desirable to assist in the organization of a constitutional assembly in which the representatives of the Japanese people can themselves draw up and accept a democratic constitution to replace the present undemocratic document given to them by their Emperor.

The United Nations should take measures to remove control of working capital from the hands of the industrial monopolists and to assist in initiating long overdue agrarian reforms. Economic assistance should be offered to Japan only in such a way that her postwar economic development can be integrated with economic reconstruction throughout the Pacific area and be made to contribute to recovery of the Far Eastern areas which Japan has devastated.

The United Nations should inaugurate a program of cultural co-operation embracing Japan and all Asiatic countries, so that exchange of information and co-operation in all fields of human activity can be rapidly increased as a basis for that mutual understanding between peoples which underlies peaceful relations. As a first step in this direction, the United Nations should reopen Japan to unrestricted access to the world's knowledge and to uncensored communication with other nations. Maintenance of this freedom should be made a condition of the re-establishment of relations between any postwar Japanese government and individual members of the United Nations.

Finally, it is essential for the United Nations to avoid any implication of racial discrimination against the Japanese. Military forces occupying Japan should include troops from all of the United Nations, Asiatic and Occidental alike, and occupation authorities should be equally representative. Wherever possible, the United Nations should apply to Japan the same treatment accorded Germany, in order to avoid charges of discrimination on racial grounds by the Japanese or any other Asiatic peoples. As a corollary to this policy, individual members of the United Nations should act to remove from their domestic legislation, particularly their immigration laws, those provisions involving racial discriminations.

The policies summarized above are not intended to be inclusive but rather to indicate the lines of action toward a postwar Japan best calculated to prevent a revival of Japanese aggression, and, what is more important, to give the Japanese people an opportunity to develop a stake in their future as a small but relatively prosperous nation and eventually to gain admission as a full member of the international community. There is no guarantee that these proposed measures, or similar ones, will achieve the desired objectives, but unless a comprehensive, constructive United Nations policy is attempted, there is the very grave risk that an unchanged

Japan will refuse to accept her lesser status and will renew her bid for power and domination at the first opportunity.

It must be emphasized that decisions relating to the future of Japan cannot be made independently of those connected with many other Far Eastern problems confronting the United Nations. Decisions with respect to Japan must harmonize with those concerning other areas in order that they do not retard or conflict with the general objective of postwar United Nations policy—a reconstruction of international relations to provide security and increased prosperity for all peoples.

Control of Japan to prevent rearmament must be related directly to the organization and operations of the United Nations security system and to eventual agreement concerning the regulation of armaments among all nations. Reconquest of the colonial areas must be accompanied by agreement among the western nations on progressive development of self-government for colonial peoples if Japan's program of 'Asia for the Asiatics' is to be finally repudiated instead of retaining a latent appeal upon which the Japanese can capitalize at a future date.

Japan's postwar economic development must be integrated into a viable system of international economic relations beneficial to all nations. Specific limitations on Japan's economy, such as reparations, as well as the terms of Japan's future economic relations with individual members of the United Nations must be co-ordinated with general agreements reached by the United Nations on such problems as currency stabilization, access to raw materials, trade arrangements, national and international investment policies, and shipping and civil air transport.

Participation of the Soviet Union in the consideration of Japan's future and other Far Eastern problems is an obvious necessity regardless of the way in which the Soviet Union may share in the final defeat of Japan. China's relations with the Soviet Union and the degree to which China attains internal political unity and develops her economic strength will indicate the amount of responsibility she can assume and the proportionate share of responsibility other United Nations must assume for maintenance of peace and for economic reconstruction in the Pacific area.

Because the United States is the most powerful nation in the Pacific area, a special duty is imposed upon the American government and the American people to accept the responsibility that goes with their predominant power and to participate fully with other United Nations in determining Japan's future and in constructing a durable peace system. But such a policy by the United States is also required because America has a special concern in the postwar treatment of Japan, a concern that arises from the past nature of Japanese-American relations.

Americans must learn that Japan considers this country her number one enemy. For in spite of the global nature of this war, in the Far East it is more nearly a grudge-fight between Japan and America, a culmination of conflicting policies over a thirty-five-year period during which the Japanese convinced themselves that it was the United States, more than any other nation, that stood in the way of fulfilment of their ambition to dominate Asia.

Since 1905, there has been almost continuous friction between Japan and the United States over such vital issues as immigration, relations with China, and naval supremacy in the Pacific. Between 1905 and 1941, tension rose and subsided, but at no time was the 'traditional friendship,' so much talked about by after-dinner speakers and good-will emissaries, strong enough to secure a definitive settlement of the major conflicting issues. On the contrary, the policies of the two nations continued along divergent lines, and their common interests lessened with the final clash of armed force as the inevitable result.

On the eve of Pearl Harbor, the Japanese could look back upon more than a quarter of a century in which actions of the United States had caused growing irritations. The Japanese could recall a series of half-won victories which might have netted them much more in prestige and power had not the United States acted in a way which they regarded as unwarranted interference with their just aims and actions. The ink was scarcely dry on the Portsmouth Treaty of 1905, which through American good offices had brought Japan to a successful end of her war with Russia, when agitation on the west coast of the United States over Japanese immigration created a Japanese antagonism toward this country which remained a barrier to adjustment of other problems and an issue on which Japan's extreme nationalists could always rally their people against America.

After the outbreak of the First World War, in 1915 the United States was mainly responsible, through diplomacy and publicity, in reducing Japan's expected gains from her Twenty-one Demands upon China. In 1918, the American decision to participate with other Allied nations, including Japan, in the Siberian intervention was largely responsible for preventing seizure of eastern Siberia and Manchuria by Japan's militarists who desired to take advantage of the Russian revolution and the breakdown of Russian authority in eastern Asia. At the Paris Peace Conference, it was an American President, Woodrow Wilson, who blocked Japan's demand for acceptance of the principle of racial equality in the League of Nations Covenant. American initiative was responsible for Japan's reluctant acceptance of an inferior naval ratio at the Washington Conference of 1922 and for Japan's assumption of the obligations to respect China's territorial integrity and the Open Door in China, two principles of American Far Eastern policy embodied in the Nine Power Treaty of the Washington Conference. After the invasion of Manchuria in 1931, Japan's militarists and their civilian supporters blamed the United States for the rebukes administered by the League of Nations in 1932 and 1937 and by the abortive Brussels Conference in the latter year. They charged America with attempts to humiliate Japan before the world, a charge for which they could mobilize considerable home support because of continued Japanese anger over the passage of the American immigration act of 1924 which discriminated against Asiatics.

This long series of actions by the United States, while only serving to check Japanese policies, nevertheless steadily increased the Japanese feeling of frustration at their powerful American neighbor across the Pacific whose policy of strong words and cautious action was at least effective enough to make the carrying forward of Japanese expansion more difficult. Time and again, largely by diplomatic action, the United States had been instrumental in preventing Japan from securing everything she was after at the moment. American actions were partially successful in limiting and on a few occasions in reducing Japan's gains, but not in changing Japan's ambitions and ultimate goals. That the United States continued to oppose a peace in Asia 'made in Japan' but was unwilling to enforce a peace 'made in America' not only was hard for the Japanese to understand because of their militaristic traditions; it also became a positive and a growing irritant in their relations with America. As the Japanese militarists and extreme nationalists gained in power at home, as they proceeded with their Asiatic conquests against no more than verbal American opposition, their desire to end American 'interference' with their 'immutable' policies increased to the point where war with the United States seemed to them both necessary and possible of victorious conclusion.

On the American side, feeling against Japan has blown hot and cold and often has been localized on the West Coast. Few Americans tried to understand Japanese feelings or the dangers inherent in growing Japanese antagonism to their country's policies. Few Americans thought that Japan would risk war with the United States. This was due largely to official American silence on the gravity of the issues between the two nations and to the government's lack of public warning of Japan's will to fight. For example, Franklin D. Roosevelt wrote in 1923 that 'Outside the executive departments at Washington it has never been known in this country that, during the nervous days in the early summer of 1908, the United States hovered on the edge of an ultimatum from Japan.' A reading of the diplomatic correspondence so far published by the State Department reveals similar periods of tension immediately after the last war and during the decade before Pearl Harbor, but these revelations came too late to prepare the American people for the final clash of December 1941.

This brief review of Japanese-American conflict indicates the basis of Japanese antagonism toward the United States. The Japanese people were told before the war began that it was America alone that was 'blocking' the realization of Japan's 'peaceful purposes.' They were told that the efforts of their leaders to bring peace and prosperity to the Greater East Asia Sphere were succeeding except for American interference through aid to China. When the United States froze all Japanese assets in July 1941, although Great Britain and the Netherlands joined in this action, the Japanese people were told that this was just another instance of American effort to 'strangle' their country and that Britain and the Netherlands had been deceived by American 'imperialists,' who were trying to create an American empire in Asia. The Japanese people were told that the American note to Japan of November 26, 1941, which the American Government maintained was an equitable offer for adjustment of Japanese-American relations, was a clear ultimatum which their nation's honor demanded be met with war.

When Japan is defeated and the Japanese can learn the truth, they will learn that their loss of the war has been largely due to the efforts of the United States. This will fit in with what they have been told for many years and it will be natural for them to hold the United States responsible for loss of their empire, devastation to their homeland, and for all other penalties, restrictions, and humiliations arising from their defeat. The resulting intensification of Japan's long-standing conviction that the United States is their number one enemy will make United Nations decisions concerning the future of Japan a matter of paramount national security for the United States.

If Japan fails to transform herself into a peaceful and trustworthy nation, renewal of Japanese aggression will inevitably threaten the United States, and the leaders of a new Japanese bid for empire will find their most potent support in arousing their people against the nation which successfully defeated and humiliated their country in the Second World War. Therefore, the United States cannot afford to subscribe only to restrictive and unconstructive United Nations policies toward a defeated Japan. The United States must take the lead among the United Nations in giving the people in a disarmed Japan opportunity for peaceful development, an opportunity to break their autocratic, class-dominated society, and, through democratic control of their own government, an opportunity to become an acceptable member of the community of nations. Only then will the security of the United States and the security of the whole Pacific area be assured.

Index